I0814601

MARTYRS
OF THE
EUCHARIST

MARTYRS
OF THE
EUCHARIST

Stories to Inspire Eucharistic Amazement

Reverend J. Francis Sofie, OP (Mobile)

TAN Books
Gastonia, North Carolina

Nihil Obstat: Reverend Msgr. Theodore H. Hay
July 24, 2023

Imprimatur: Most Reverend Thomas J. Rodi
Archbishop of Mobile
July 24, 2023

Cover design by Jordan Avery

Cover image: The Glory of the Saints, Guercino (Giovanni Francesco Barbieri) (1591-1666). 1645, oil on canvas, Musee des Augustins, Toulouse, France / Bridgeman Images.

ISBN: 978-1-5051-3409-4
Kindle ISBN: 978-1-5051-3468-1
ePUB ISBN: 978-1-5051-3467-4

Published in the United States by
TAN Books
PO Box 269
Gastonia, NC 28053
www.TANBooks.com

Printed in India

To Saint Joseph:
Guardian of the Bread of Life
Adorer of the Word made Flesh
Spiritual Father of Priests

CONTENTS

Part Two: Those Martyred in Defense or Protection of the Most Blessed Sacrament

Part Three: Those Who Risked Their Lives for the Most Blessed Sacrament

Part Four: Other Deaths Connected with the Most Blessed Sacrament

INTRODUCTION

THERE is nothing more amazing in this life than the Holy Eucharist. Nothing. No exception. This statement is not hyperbole. This is an objective fact. No miracle of physical healing as at Lourdes, no dancing Sun as at Fatima, no liquification of blood as in St. Januarius compares with the sublime and inexhaustible mystery of the Most Holy Eucharist. As such, every believer should be filled with "Eucharistic amazement." This was an expression taken from Pope St. John Paul II's last encyclical entitled *Ecclesia de Eucharistia*, dated Holy Thursday, April 17, AD 2003.

The Holy Father reminds all the faithful that the Eucharist makes present the once-in-time Paschal Mystery that is now for all times. The opening statement of his last encyclical declares: "The Church draws her life from the Eucharist." Perhaps no one appreciates this more than the men and women who preferred physical death rather than betray the source of life available in the Most Holy Eucharist. We call these men and women "martyrs of the Eucharist." And their witness ought to inspire in us Eucharistic amazement.

The word "martyr" comes from a Greek word meaning "witness." Its theological significance denotes that a martyr renders the definitive and perfect witness of his faith in Jesus Christ, who offered His own life for our salvation. Jesus gives us Himself so we can live wholly for Him and, if He so wills, give Him our very life with the confidence that, in surrendering our natural life, we will find a life of unending happiness with Him (see Mk 8:35).

To witness for Jesus, though, is not merely to speak in defense of Him; it is not sufficient merely to call Him "Lord" (see Mt 7:21). In addition to our public profession of Jesus's lordship, we must live our lives in a manner that they too bear witness to Jesus's lordship. A Christian's witness of Jesus must be an authentic and integral witness: his words, his actions, his values, his very life must bear the imprint of Jesus. A Christian's life, if lived authentically, will be a "sign of contradiction" (see Lk 2:34) in a world that is at enmity with the Person and the values of Jesus Christ.

The principle of Christian witness is simple but challenging: as Jesus gave all for us, so we must give all for Him. Christian witness is a call to self-donation, of surrendering all that we are to the One who created us, who died and rose for us, and who brings us into communion with Himself through the Paschal Mystery. Nothing, therefore, is ever so important that it mitigates a Christian's obligation to witness to Jesus, not even preserving his own life (see Mt 16:25). The nature of the Gospel of Jesus is that it can never be compromised. Jesus calls for a whole-hearted commitment to Him and His Gospel. Martyrs are those men, women, and children who prefer death to compromise; they prefer integrity to duplicity. But this commitment to Jesus, this willingness to lay down one's life for Him, is possible only because a person *first* lived for Him. Red martyrdom (to shed one's blood for faith in Jesus) flows from white martyrdom (to live each day for Jesus).

In the history of the Church, there have been martyrs for many aspects of the Catholic faith. St. Peter (+AD 64) and St. Paul (+AD 67) were martyred because they professed the lordship and divinity of Jesus Christ and would not bend their knee to an impostor. St. Felicity (+c. AD 201) was martyred for her faith in Jesus, her refusal to worship a false god, and her refusal to prefer safety with her father rather than to renounce her Savior. St. Cecilia (+c. AD 230), like

St. Peter and St. Paul, refused to worship a false god, and her fidelity resulted in her execution by the sword. St. Thomas More (+AD 1535) was a martyr for the sacramentality and the indissolubility of marriage. St. Josaphat (+AD 1623) was a martyr for the supremacy of the Bishop of Rome. Blessed Miguel Pro (+AD 1927) was martyred because he was a priest who ministered to the people though it was against the civil law in Mexico.

In this book, I consider the lives of men and women who were martyrs of a very specific aspect of the Catholic faith: the Holy Eucharist. This great Sacrament of the Eucharist is "the source and summit of the Christian life."[1] Since the Eucharist is Jesus Christ Himself, to die for the Eucharist is to die for Jesus Christ, who said of Himself, "I am the bread of life" (Jn 6:35) and, "He who loses his life for my sake will find it" (Mt 10:39).

Recently, on the solemnity of Corpus Christi, I was led to preach on Martyrs of the Eucharist. In doing research for this homily, to my surprise, I discovered there was no book dedicated to this important subject. I believe this is a significant lacuna that needs addressing.

This book treats the Martyrs of the Eucharist in four divisions. Part One relates the heroic stories of priests who were killed for celebrating the Holy Sacrifice of the Mass or the laity who were killed while attending the Mass. Part Two considers those men and women who fearlessly died defending or protecting the Eucharist. Part Three recounts the remarkable stories of persons who risked their lives for the Eucharist, though they were not actually killed. And Part Four describes the remarkable stories of those who died because of some intimate connection to the Eucharist.

There is a theological connection between martyrdom and the Eucharist. The Church teaches that the Eucharist is not a symbol; it is not a metaphor; it is not something that evokes the presence of Jesus as a memory. The Eucharist *is* the actual Real Presence of Jesus Christ. When Jesus declared at the Last Supper, while holding

[1] *Catechism of the Catholic Church,* no. 1324. Quoting LG 11.

bread, "This is my body," it became what He declared, just as when God declared, "'Let there be light,' and there was light" (Gn 1:3). The Eucharist is the fulfillment of Jesus's promise that He would be with His Church until the end of the world (see Mt 28:20). His Real Presence is His whole presence: Body, Blood, soul and divinity. The *Catechism of the Catholic Church* states: "In the most blessed sacrament of the Eucharist 'the body and blood, together with the soul and divinity, of our Lord Jesus Christ and, therefore, *the whole Christ is truly, really, and substantially* contained.'"[2]

Thus, the Eucharistic Presence is not partial; it is not incomplete; it is not half-hearted. All that Jesus is, His full divinity and His full humanity, is made an enduring gift to us in the Eucharist. He gives all to help and empower us to give all we are back to Him. Those who literally die for Jesus do this. And in offering to Jesus their very lives, they make their lives a kind of "Eucharistic sacrifice" to Him. St. Ignatius of Antioch made this comparison: "I write to the Churches, and impress on them all, that I shall willingly die for God, unless you hinder me. . . . Allow me to become food for the wild beasts, through whose instrumentality it will be granted me to attain to God. I am the wheat of God, and let me be ground by the teeth of the wild beasts, that I may be found the pure bread of Christ. . . . Then shall I truly be a disciple of Christ. . . . Entreat Christ for me, that by these instruments I may be found a sacrifice to God."[3] Martyrdom is therefore a Eucharistic act. The Eucharist pours into us a share in the selfless and sacrificial love that animated Jesus in His passion.

In writing this book and sharing the witness of these heroic men and women over the centuries, it is my hope and prayer that we too will have a martyr's faith with respect to the Eucharist and grow in

---

2 *Catechism of the Catholic Church,* no. 1374, quoting the Council of Trent (1551).

3 St. Ignatius, *Epistle to the Romans,* chapter 4, accessed February 20, 2024, https://www.newadvent.org/fathers/0107.htm.

our Eucharistic amazement of so great a sacrament. If the Eucharist is Jesus Christ Himself, then what is more important to our relationship with Him than this Sacrament? The Eucharist must be central to our lives since Jesus must be central. He must make a difference, and so the Eucharist must make a difference in how we live. Sadly, according to a survey by the Center for Applied Research in the Apostolate, only about 24 percent of Catholics in the United States regularly attend the Mass. Spiritually speaking, as Catholics, we cannot absent ourselves from His Eucharistic Presence and expect to persevere in the life of grace. As the "source and summit of the Christian life," we need the Eucharist in order to live spiritually, just as we need air to breathe and food to eat to live physically. But we are made for more than physical existence; we are made to live in a communion of love that is the very heart of the Trinity. And the Eucharist gives us a share in this heart of love.

May the Martyrs of the Eucharist pray for us that we rediscover Jesus Christ, truly present in the Holy Eucharist. May we go to meet Him in the Eucharist, never missing an opportunity to be with Him. May we open our hearts to His Real Presence and thereby become transformed more perfectly into His image.

Praised be Jesus Christ in the Most Blessed Sacrament of the Altar!

Part One

Those Martyred for Celebrating or Attending the Holy Mass

Chapter 1
POPE SAINT SIXTUS II

Martyred August 6, AD 258
Rome, Italy

PRIOR to becoming the emperor of the Roman Empire, Valerian, who reigned as emperor from AD 253–260, was apparently responsible for, or at least intimately involved in, the persecution of the Church under Emperor Decius (reigned AD 249–251). Decius specifically targeted the leadership of the Church. His rationale was that if the head is severed, then the body will die quickly. Bishops, priests, and deacons were sought out to offer sacrifice to the pagan gods; among those who died in this persecution was Pope Saint Fabian (reigned AD 236–250).

When Valerian became emperor two years after the death of Decius, it was thus no surprise that he resumed a program of fierce persecution. In AD 257, Valerian ordered bishops and priests to offer sacrifice to the pagan gods or face exile. Additionally, this decree forbade gathering in cemeteries, an obvious attempt to purge Rome and the empire from the celebration of the Holy Mass. The following year, Valerian intensified the penalty from exile to execution. It was in this second phase of persecution that Pope Saint Sixtus II was martyred on August 6, AD 258.

Saint Sixtus II was elected the twenty-fourth pope on August 2, AD 257. To keep his election in context, every preceding pope died a martyr's death. One year and four days after he became the Bishop of Rome, Sixtus II, together with several deacons, gathered in a lesser-known cemetery, that of Praetextatus, located off the Appian Way, for the celebration of the Holy Sacrifice of the Mass. Sixtus knew his life was in jeopardy, but not to celebrate the Holy Mass, and thereby be deprived of the Holy Eucharist, was a far greater suffering.

On August 6, AD 258, a few days after Valerian issued his second decree and intensified the penalty from exile to death, Pope Sixtus and four deacons gathered for the Mass. At some point in the Mass, while Sixtus was seated, soldiers of the Roman Empire descended upon the pope and his deacons. Either Sixtus was instantly killed while seated or he was taken to the city for a perfunctory hearing and returned to the cemetery, where he was promptly martyred by decapitation.

Pope St. Sixtus II is memorialized in the First Eucharistic Prayer, also known as the Roman Canon, in the list of early martyrs of the Church.

Reflection

Though this martyrdom occurred over seventeen hundred years ago, it is for us an eloquent and perennially pertinent homily preached by the example of our Holy Father about the supreme importance of the Holy Eucharist. Jesus taught us in the Gospel of St. John, chapter 6, that the Eucharist communicates supernatural life to us and that those who participate in this Sacrament of divine life and love will live forever. "I am the living bread which came down from heaven; if any one eats of this bread, he will live for ever; and the bread which I shall give for the life of the world is my flesh" (Jn 6:51–52). Pope Sixtus offered his life to the One whose life makes us a new creation. He now enjoys this life of beatitude forever.

Through his example, the Holy Father reminds us today that, no matter the personal inconvenience, nothing should keep us from the Eucharist. We may not personally like the priest-celebrant or his homily or the style of music or the architecture of the church, but none of that should keep us from the Eucharist, the source of life. Pope Saint Sixtus did not let the threat of death keep him from the Mass. What is keeping us from the Greatest Gift imaginable?

Chapter 2

Saint Edmund Gennings, Saint Polydore Plasden, Saint Swithin Wells, Blessed Sydney Hodgson, Blessed John Mason, and Blessed Brian Lacey

Martyred December 10, AD 1591
London, England

THE name "Richard Topcliffe" may not be well-known to contemporary Catholics, but in England in the late sixteenth century, every Catholic knew and feared him. Officially, he was Queen Elizabeth I's "interrogator." The innocuous title, though, masked his real nefarious and sadistic activities and his solitary obsession in life: the utter eradication of the Catholic faith in England. He was a "priest-hunter" at a time when in England simply being a priest was classified as high treason, punishable by a horrific death: to be hanged, drawn, and quartered.

His absolute hatred for practicing Catholics was well-known and documented; he had nothing less than an avaricious appetite for priests in particular but also for "recusants," Catholics who refused to embrace the "Established church." To extract information from captured priests and lay Catholics who were suspected of harboring these enemies of the state, the Machiavellian Topcliffe subjected them to unspeakable tortures. Some victims of his torture gave up the desired information to Topcliffe, or they embraced the Established church, but most preferred torture and death to betraying priests or renouncing their cherished Catholic faith. As an illustration of the zeal and even glee with which Topcliffe performed his atrocious responsibilities, he constructed a torture chamber in his private residence and devised a method of torture that he said made the rack seem like "child's play" in comparison. He personally oversaw the execution of countless priests and laypeople. Records indicate that if a particular priest angered him excessively, such as Father Edmund Gennings, Topcliffe found a way to intensify the priest's torture and prolong the dying process to enhance his own perverse pleasure.

Richard Topcliffe worked fiendishly to discover the names and locations of all priests in England. He would not rest until the country was eradicated of this cancer called Catholicism. Father Edmund Gennings was of particular interest to Topcliffe because Gennings, at fourteen years of age, abandoned the Established church in order to become Catholic. Shortly after Gennings's reception into the Catholic Church, he began studies to become a priest. He studied at Douai College in France and was ordained a priest of Jesus Christ on March 18, AD 1590; he was twenty-three years old at his ordination and therefore had to receive a dispensation due to his young age.

In April, AD 1590, Father Gennings set sail for his beloved country of England in order to nourish the faith of his fellow Catholics through the sacraments, most especially with the Most Holy Eucharist. Father Gennings served as a priest in London for slightly over one year before Topcliffe apprehended him while he was celebrating the Holy Mass. Before his capture, Father Gennings donned disguises and in secret administered the sacraments to Catholics. A network developed throughout England whereby faithful Catholics hid priests in their homes in order to avoid their apprehension. Nicholas Owen, a Jesuit brother, himself a martyr for hiding priests, is credited with constructing countless "priest holes," as they were called; some may still be undiscovered, so talented was he.

On November 2, AD 1591, on the second floor of the home of Swithin Wells, Father Gennings arrived for the celebration of the Mass. He was accompanied by Father Polydore Plasden. In attendance were Sydney Hogdson, John Mason, and Brian Lacey. Swithin Wells, though not present for the Mass, offered his home for Mass on several occasions; his wife was in attendance. Richard Topcliffe and officers descended on the house in the hopes of finding "papists" engaged in the "repugnant" and "superstitious" ceremony called the Mass. They actually arrived while the Mass was in progress and unexpectedly burst into the room. John Mason struggled with Richard Topcliffe to prevent his entrance and any profanation of the Mass or attack on the priest; Topcliffe fell backwards down the stairs and the others quickly barred the door long enough for Father Gennings to conclude the Mass. Topcliffe cut his head in the fall down the stairs and was livid. He swore Father Gennings would pay dearly for his crime of celebrating the Holy Mass.

As soon as the Sacrifice of the Mass ended, everyone went peacefully, offering no resistance and surrendering themselves to Topcliffe; Father Gennings was still vested for Mass. The day after their arrests, Swithin Wells returned to his home and was immediately arrested. On December 4, the participants in the Mass were formally charged: Father Gennings with high treason, the others with a felony. Unsurprisingly, all were found guilty, the punishment being death; Swithin's wife was apparently given life imprisonment as a concession. Topcliffe personally escorted Father Gennings to his place of confinement and offered him his life if he simply embraced the Established church. Without hesitation, Father Gennings refused the offer. This infuriated Topcliffe, who then ordered Gennings to be transferred to what was called "the Little Ease." The Little Ease was a four-foot room, without windows, and due to its size, it prevented the detainee to stand erect, sit, or lie down; the only posture was to crouch; it caused excruciating agony with each passing moment. Father Gennings endured this agony for six days without relief.

On December 10, AD 1591, Topcliffe took Father Gennings and Swithin Wells to Wells's house for their public execution. Topcliffe again renewed his offer of clemency if they renounced their Catholic faith, and again both refused. Father Gennings was sentenced to be hanged, drawn, and quartered. To intensify Father Gennings's torment, Topcliffe ordered Gennings to be prematurely cut down from hanging because he did not want Gennings to lose any of the painful sensations that come with being drawn and quartered. Stretched out, as a lamb led to the slaughter, the executioner began to disembowel Father Gennings, even to the point of removing his beating heart. Father Gennings chose death rather than life because he knew that physical death was his entry into a life of unending joy and happiness.

Immediately after Father Gennings's martyrdom, Swithin Wells was hanged until he died. Father Polydore Plasden was martyred on the same day but at Tyburn by hanging; his original sentence was the same as Father Gennings, but Sir Walter Raleigh ordered that he be permitted to die by hanging and that the remainder of the sentence be carried out on his corpse. Also hanged at Tyburn were Brian Lacey, Sydney Hodgdon, and John Mason; the latter was also drawn and quartered.

Father Gennings, Father Polydore Plasden, and Swithin Wells were canonized on October 25, AD 1970, by Pope Paul VI. Brian Lacey, John Mason, and Sydney Hodgson were beatified by Pope Pius XI on December 15, AD 1929.

The great Christian apologist and theologian Tertullian famously wrote that the blood of the martyrs is the seed of Christianity.[4] At

---

4 Tertullian, *Apologia* 50, accessed February 22, 2024, https://www.newadvent.org/fathers/0301.htm.

Father Gennings's execution and martyrdom stood his brother, John, a member of the Established church, though only nominally so. John Gennings's life to that point was dedicated to pursuing his own pleasures. Initially, John writes in a biography of his brother that he welcomed his brother's death since John otherwise would not be free from his Catholic influence. Ten days after Edmund's death, John had a spiritual experience whereby he immediately recognized the beauty of sanctity in the lives of the saints, most especially the Queen of all Saints, Our Lady. It was a special grace, no doubt, that his brother obtained for him as St. Stephen merited the conversion of Saul. John felt a burning desire in his heart to learn everything about the Faith which his brother so willingly and heroically died for. He was received into the Catholic Church and shortly thereafter entered seminary to become a priest. Ordained in AD 1607, he soon developed a wish to see the Franciscans return to England. Father John Gennings became a Franciscan and was tasked with the responsibility and the oversight of re-founding the Franciscans in England. This he did with incredible zeal and commitment. He died in AD 1660.

Reflection

Do I love going to the Mass? Do I look forward to Mass? Or is it something I am obligated to do, and that is the only reason I attend? Is it something I actually dread? Do I see the Mass as a lot of fuss, a lot of empty, outdated ritual with little to no significance for my life?

How we answer those questions will reflect our basic understanding of what the Mass is in itself. The Holy Sacrifice of the Mass is so much more than what most people think. In fact, there can be no greater act of worship we can render the living God than our participation in the Mass, and that is in spite of poor homilies, poor music, poor architecture, and distractions. The heart of the Mass is the self-offering of the Son to the Father through the Holy Spirit;

the self-offering is identical to the self-offering on Calvary. It is not another self-offering; it is that exact same self-offering that the liturgy permits access to throughout the ages. If the question were put this way: Would you, if you could, be present with Jesus while He accomplished our salvation on Calvary? What Christian would say "No" to this? And yet that is the reality of the Mass. How can we, therefore, prefer anything else to this? What can be greater than to be with Jesus in the greatest act of love the world has ever known?

Chapter 3
SAINT JOHN ROBERTS, OSB

Martyred December 10, AD 1610
London, England

ON the nineteenth anniversary of the martyrdom of St. Edmund Gennings, St. Polydore Plasden, St. Swithin Wells, Bl. Sydney Hodgson, Bl. John Mason, and Bl. Brian Lacey, another martyr of the Eucharist, caught in the act of celebrating the Mass, was executed; he was a convert to the Catholic faith and a Benedictine monk and priest, John Roberts.

John studied at St. John's College in Oxford, though he did not complete the degree. He left England and eventually went to France, where he was immersed in Catholicism and became Catholic in AD 1598 at Notre Dame in Paris. From France, John traveled to Spain, where he joined the Benedictine Abbey in Valladolid. John was sent to the Abbey of Saint Martin in Compostela to make his novitiate, and in AD 1600, he made his religious profession as a Benedictine. After further study, John was ordained at the Abbey to the priesthood of Jesus Christ.

Shortly after John's ordination, he experienced a burning desire to return to his native land to minister, especially in light of the plague that was ravishing London at the time. To return to England, though, could mean horrendous torture and a grisly death if caught.

Despite that threat, Father John returned as a missionary to England in AD 1603. What then follows in the life of John Roberts, from AD 1603 until his martyrdom in AD 1610, is an incredible series of six different arrests and four subsequent banishments.

After arriving in April, AD 1603, he was arrested and exiled in May, AD 1603. He returned the following year only to be caught shortly thereafter and again exiled. His third arrest occurred in AD 1605, when he was imprisoned for seven months and then exiled in AD 1606. (Father John was arrested in the company of Thomas Percy's wife. Thomas was a co-conspirator in the infamous AD 1605 Gunpowder plot, a failed attempt to assassinate King James I by blowing up Parliament when the King was scheduled to be present.) The determined Father John returned to London in October AD 1607, only to be arrested two months later in December; he was imprisoned at the Gatehouse prison but managed to escape and he ministered in London clandestinely for another year. In AD 1609, Father John was apprehended and sentenced to die in May; the French ambassador, Antoine de la Broderie, however, intervened on his behalf and secured a commutation of the sentence to his fourth banishment.

Only a few months elapsed from this banishment when Father John returned for what would be his last time. A former priest who became an informant for the English government, John Cecil, reported to officials the whereabouts of Father John. As Father John was concluding the celebration of the Holy Sacrifice of the Mass, he was arrested and led away while still vested; he was convicted on December 5 and executed on December 10, AD 1610 at Tyburn Tree in London, the same location where St. Edmund Campion was martyred in AD 1581.

Father John Roberts, because he was guilty of ministering as a Catholic priest, received the usual sentence: he was to be hanged, drawn, and quartered. The sentence typically entailed that after a person was hanged, but before death, he would be cut down from the gallows, and the executioner would proceed to disembowel the condemned while still alive. At Father John's execution, the gathered crowd opposed this treatment of this beloved priest who risked his life so many times to minister to the plague victims. The executioner acquiesced to the crowd, and he ensured Father John's death prior to disembowelment. He was thirty-three years old.

Father John Roberts, OSB, was canonized by Pope Paul VI on October 25, AD 1970, as one of the Forty Martyrs of England and Wales.

Reflection

Perhaps the most outstanding virtue evidenced in the life of St. John Roberts was his sheer determination that not even the threat of death would keep him from ministering to the physical and spiritual needs of Londoners. St. John's determination must have been more than natural at its source; it must have been supernatural, inspired by a keen penetration into the mystery of divine love.

The Holy Eucharist is the Sacrament of divine love since the Eucharist makes present to us the prodigious love of Jesus Christ on the Cross. The world has not, nor will it ever, know a greater love than this: God becoming man so that He can in His very flesh manifest the love He has for each of us. Each participation in the Sacrifice of the Mass, each worthy reception of the Blessed Sacrament, immerses the communicant into this mystery of divine love, a love that seeks to share love with others. St. John was animated by the intensity of divine love in the Eucharist, and this fired his determination to bring Christ's love and mercy to those in most need. Love for Father John was not a mere sentiment but the supernatural impetus originating in his devotion to the Blessed Sacrament and manifesting itself in his priestly ministry. Divine love is a love that reaches out to the other. St. John literally died putting this love into action.

Are we determined to share the love of Christ Jesus with others? Do we share with others the beauty of the Holy Eucharist? Do we share with others the love that is the Holy Eucharist? Have we invited people of other faiths to come with us to the Mass? Do our lives reflect the life-giving, self-donating, sacrificial love we receive in the Eucharist? Is the Eucharist making our lives more loving and less selfish?

Chapter 4

Blessed William Southerne

Martyred April 30, AD 1618
Newcastle-upon-Tyne, England

IN the Mass of ordination to the sacred priesthood, the bishop presents to the newly ordained priest the gifts of bread and wine brought forth by the people of God. The gesture denotes the principal priestly ministry to offer the Sacrifice of the Mass under the appearance of bread and wine for the salvation of others and the worship of almighty God. The Sacrifice of the Mass bridges both time and distance: (1) it brings the past event of Calvary into the eternal "now" of liturgical time; and (2) it transports the participants to the foot of the Cross at Calvary to be present for the once-in-time-sacrifice-that-is-now-for-all-time. Furthermore, the Mass parts the veil of heaven and ushers the worshippers into the eternal liturgy of the Son offering Himself to the Father through the Holy Spirit.

In the Mass of Ordination, as the bishop presents the bread and wine, he says to the new priest, "Receive the oblation of the holy people, to be offered to God. Understand what you do, imitate what you celebrate, and conform your life to the mystery of the Lord's cross."

Baptism conforms the baptized to God the Son; what Jesus is by nature, the Son of God, is sacramentally communicated to the baptized by His grace. Ordination to the priesthood conforms the priest to Jesus, the Suffering and Crucified Servant. A priest's life and ministry without the Cross figuring prominently reflects a diminished priesthood. As his ordination configured him to Jesus, the Suffering and Crucified Servant, so the intentional embrace of suffering in his life manifests his acceptance of what and who he has become. Priesthood can no more exist without suffering than Jesus, in His sacred humanity, could fulfill the Father's will without it.

This truism about the priesthood is powerfully revealed in the lives and the self-offering of the priest-martyrs. Most priests, though, are not called to literal martyrdom but all are called to spiritual martyrdom. Blessed William Southerne certainly embodied this mystical and essential dimension of who he became through ordination to the priesthood of Jesus Christ. In the words from the Order of Ordination, his life was conformed to "the mystery of the Lord's cross."

Little is known about the life of William Southerne. He was born around AD 1569 in Ketton, County Durham, England. He studied for the priesthood in France and Spain and was ordained to the sacred priesthood in Spain. Upon his ordination, Father Southerne returned to his native land to minister to clandestine Catholics; he did so with great zeal for fourteen years before his identity as a priest was revealed to the government. While celebrating the Holy Sacrifice of the Mass, Father Southerne was apprehended and led off while still vested for Mass. Simply being a priest was a treasonous act per the Jesuits, etc., Act of 1584. After his arrest, the accused had the opportunity to take an oath of loyalty to the English monarch, which included the acknowledgement and acceptance of the monarch's spiritual authority over all English Christians; refusal to do so was punishable by torture and death.

Such was the fate that awaited Father Southerne, who refused to take the oath, an oath that necessitated he deny his Catholic faith. Wearing his vestments for Holy Mass, the evidence was incontrovertible, and Father Southerne was found guilty of being a priest. His sentence was to be executed by being hanged almost to death, eviscerated, and then beheaded. Father William Southerne underwent this horrific martyrdom for celebrating the Holy Mass, thereby sealing his ultimate configuration to the Suffering and Crucified Jesus on April 30, AD 1618.

Father William Southerne was beatified by Pope St. John Paul II on November 18, AD 1987, as one of eighty-five Martyrs of England and Wales. Their feast is May 4.

Reflection

Blessed William Southerne became a priest and ministered in England at a time when to do so carried an almost certain death sentence if discovered. Imagine embracing a vocation in which death for that vocation was a very real possibility. Would we nevertheless accept and follow that vocation out of love for God and His most holy will? Yet such a reality did not dissuade Blessed William Southerne. What compelled him was a love for Truth; not truth in an abstract, philosophical sense, but Truth as the incarnate Son of God. It was his love for Jesus, as the Way and the Truth and the Life, that motivated him to unhesitatingly accept God's vocation for his life, regardless of potential suffering. It was his love for the holy and apostolic Faith that compelled him since England had departed from this Faith. Souls were at risk; the integrity of the Faith "once for all delivered to the saints" (Jude 1:3) was in jeopardy. God destined Father William Southerne to play a pivotal role in preaching the truth of the Gospel, in reconciling lapsed Catholics, and ultimately to give witness to the centrality of the Holy Sacrifice of the Mass in the life of the Church and for the life of the world. Father Southerne's witness is a reminder to pray for holy vocations to the priesthood; to pray for laity and the ordained who are charged with the handing on of the Faith; to pray for those who are actively being persecuted for the holy Catholic and apostolic Faith.

Chapter 5

Blessed Thomas (John Baptist) Bullaker, OFM

Martyred October 12, AD 1642
London, England

FATHER John Baptist Bullaker was about to begin the beautiful prayer in the Mass that was inspired by the angelic chorus on the first Christmas night: the Gloria. At that moment, Father John Baptist, who received a vision two years previously of his arrest and martyrdom, was apprehended by a priest-hunter and dragged away still vested for Mass. It was September 11, AD 1642; he had been betrayed for five pieces of gold by a maid who tended the house in which he often celebrated Mass. For many people, the reality of being arrested for being a Catholic priest would be accompanied by a sense of dread, since the penalty for this "crime" was certain death. But Father John Baptist had actively prayed for this grace of martyrdom. Hence, that he was apprehended at the Gloria seems a fitting moment, for now he was to glorify God through his martyrdom.

Thomas Bullaker was born in Midhurst, Sussex, England, in either AD 1603 or AD 1604. Both his mother and father were devout Catholics; his father was a successful medical doctor. Thomas traveled to France for academic studies. While in France, he discerned a religious vocation to the Franciscans and entered the order in AD 1622, receiving the name "John Baptist." He was ordained to the holy priesthood about AD 1627.

Though his initial desire was to be assigned as a missionary to the West Indies, his superior missioned him to England. Father John Baptist landed in Plymouth to begin his missionary activity among his countrymen and was promptly arrested; due to insufficient evidence of his crime, he was released. The following twelve years saw a fruitful ministry by Father John Baptist. He donned various disguises to avoid capture. Ministering as a Catholic priest was still classified as high treason, punishable by death by means of being hanged, drawn, and quartered. Despite this threat, Father John Baptist laid aside concerns for his life that he might bring the grace of the sacraments to his brothers and sisters in Christ. Eternal life and fidelity to Jesus and His Church, not life in this world with its allure of wealth, pleasure, and safety, were his principal motivations. He knew personally how the sacraments, especially the greatest of all the sacraments, the Most Holy Eucharist, were absolutely vital to his spiritual well-being; how could he put personal safety and comfort above the need Catholics have of receiving the sacraments? Jesus assured His disciples that one of the effects of the Sacrament of His precious Body and Blood was eternal life. For this reason, Father John Baptist was ordained. This was his *raison d'etre*.

At his trial for the crime of ministering as a Catholic priest, Father John Baptist spoke in his own defense. He admitted to being a priest and ministering as a priest, but he vehemently denied this meant he was treasonous. Father John Baptist demonstrated that one can be both a good and practicing Catholic and priest and be a faithful and devoted son of the crown; they were not mutually exclusive, but actually the former allowed him to excel at the latter. The jury wavered, which prompted the judge to intervene, fearing the jury was on the verge of acquitting Father John Baptist. The judge found him guilty of high treason and sentenced him to death by hanging and being drawn and quartered. In his heart, Father John Baptist thanked God, and prayed his death would glorify Him and draw others to embrace the Church of His Son.

Father John Baptist was taken to Tyburn, where many brother priests before him had won the crown of martyrdom. Prior to his execution, Father John Baptist took the opportunity to preach his final sermon; to all those who came to witness his death, he shared the gift and the beauty of the priesthood of Jesus Christ and the Real Presence of Jesus in the Sacrament of the Altar. The Real Presence, he probably said, was precisely what Jesus said it was, His real Body and it was the Thirty-Nine Articles of Anglicanism that departed from the express will of Jesus. Father John Baptist was ordered to be silent; he complied, knowing his death itself would speak the truth of the Eucharist.

The hangman put the noose around Father John Baptist's neck, tightened it, and then the order came for him to hang. Before he was allowed to die, he was cut down, and the executioner began to cut into his still living, breathing body, excising his beating heart. Father John Baptist united his life and his death with that of Jesus. He died about thirty-eight years of age on October 12, AD 1642.

Pope John Paul II beatified Father Thomas (John Baptist) Bullaker on November 22, AD 1987, with eighty-four other martyrs of the Faith.

Reflection

St. Pio of Pietrelcina is credited with saying, "It would be easier for the world to exist without the sun, than for it to exist without the Mass." Do we truly believe this? Do we, in as much as we can, understand what happens in the Holy Mass? What graces are afforded us through the Mass? Is the Mass, and therefore the Eucharist, the center of our lives, as it was for Blessed Thomas Bullaker?

Do we make plans with the realization that Mass on Sunday (or Saturday evening) is the highest priority and nothing should displace it?

The world revolves around the sun, but do our lives revolve around the Son in the Eucharist? Are we in practice "Eucharistically centered"? Does devotion to the Eucharist inform all dimensions of our lives? Are we caviler about attending and participating in "the mystery of our Faith"? Is the Holy Eucharist the very "source and summit" of our lives?

Chapter 6

SERVANT OF GOD LEO HEINRICHS, OFM

Martyred February 23, AD 1908
Denver, Colorado

FROM the beginning of Joseph Heinrichs's life (August 15, AD 1867, in Germany) until his martyrdom (February 23, AD 1908, Denver, Colorado), he seemed to be under the protective care of Our Lady. Joseph Heinrichs, who was named for his father, was born on the great feast of Our Lady's Assumption into Heaven; that, too, was the day of his baptism, the moment he became a son of God, and the moment Mary became his mother in the order of grace. Throughout his life, Joseph was devoted to Our Lady. And she did for Joseph what she always does for those devoted to her: she took Joseph to her Son, Jesus.

Joseph's life reflected the life of Jesus more perfectly by professing the three evangelical counsels of poverty, chastity, and obedience. Joseph entered the Order of Friars Minor in Germany in AD 1886 and received the name "Leo." Due, however, to the anti-Catholic legislature of Otto von Bismarck, the first chancellor of Germany, the Franciscan community fled Germany in AD 1886 and moved to Paterson, New Jersey, to the monastery of St. Bonaventure. Joseph, now known as Brother Leo, made his final religious profession on the feast of Our Lady's Immaculate Conception (December 8, AD 1890). Leo's configuration to Christ intensified when, on the feast of Our Lady's mother, St. Anne, Brother Leo became Father Leo with his ordination to the sacred priesthood of Jesus Christ (July 26, AD 1891).

Father Leo faithfully and selflessly served the people of God and his religious community in various ways: he served St. Bonaventure parish for eleven years; he served St. Stephen's parish in Croghan, New York, in which he was tasked with the responsibility of rebuilding the parish buildings that had previously been destroyed by fire; he was reassigned again to St. Bonaventure parish as pastor; and then, in 1907, he received an assignment to go to St. Elizabeth parish in Denver, Colorado, as pastor and superior of the Franciscan community.

Father Leo was an exceptional pastor and priest; in the spirit of the founder of his religious order, St. Francis of Assisi, he too had a particular love for the poor. No one ever besought his help in vain. It was a common sight at St. Elizabeth parish to see a line of poor people seeking assistance from this gentle and gracious pastor. Additionally, Father Leo loved the children and personally taught them their catechism. No doubt Father Leo's cheerfulness and thoughtfulness endeared him to young and old alike. He was the priest that everyone loved. That is why the events of February 23, 1908, seemed all the more unbelievable and odious.

As pastor of St. Elizabeth parish, Father Leo routinely took the 8 a.m. Sunday morning Mass, while another friar took the 6 a.m. Mass. But on the evening before, Father Leo told Father Wulstan Workman, who was assigned to that Mass for February 23, that he would celebrate the early morning Mass because of a prior pastoral responsibility in the parish he wished to keep. Father Wulstan did not see Father Leo again until he was called to anoint him while he lay dying in the church, at the feet of Our Lady's statue, the victim of a bullet fired by an Italian anarchist and socialist, who publicly and proudly admitted he hated the Catholic Church and priests in particular.

On the chilly morning of February 23, AD 1908, at 6 a.m., the parish Mass began with Father Leo ringing the bell. All stood as the priest approached the main altar and began the centuries-old prayers of the Latin Mass. Unbeknownst to anyone in St. Elizabeth, a man in the third pew from the front, wearing a large winter overcoat hiding a revolver beneath his coat, came not to worship the Lord God but rather to kill His priest. He stood and sat and knelt at the appropriate times; no one knew his nefarious motives; no one suspected that this man would momentarily shoot and kill their beloved pastor.

The seemingly innocuous man was born ten years before Father Leo in Sicily; his name was Giuseppe Alio; a cobbler by profession. He married and had three children. From all reports, Alio was raised as a good Catholic, but at some point in his adult life, he became enamored with the political ideology of socialism. This ideology was denounced and condemned by the Church.[5] Alio and his friends quickly became known as troublemakers and fled Sicily for Buenos Aires; there, they devised an assassination plot to murder an Italian priest who was outspoken against those involved in socialism. While the group of agitators still lived in Buenos Aires, they learned that this Italian priest was reassigned to a parish in the United States. And so Alio, representing the group of anarchists, also traveled to the United States in search of this priest and other priests opposing socialism.

Alio's search did not yield any results in New York, where he first arrived. He then traveled to other Italian communities in the United States trying to find this priest, and again his search was fruitless. Alio then heard of a lead on the priest's whereabouts: he was in

---

5 See Pius XI, Encyclical *Quadragesimo Anno* (May 15, 1931), nos. 117, 128; Encyclical *Divini Redemptoris* (March 19, 1937), no. 58; St. John Paul II, Encyclical *Centesimus Annus* (May 1, 1991), nos. 12–13.

Denver, Colorado. Alio traveled as quickly as he could to Denver to find the priest and kill him. He would attend several Masses at different parishes, trying to familiarize himself with the priests, but none of them resembled the priest he hoped to find.

Alio found St. Elizabeth parish in January of AD 1908 and believed Father Leo to be the priest he sought who had denounced socialism. Alio was in error; Father Leo was not Italian and had not been in Sicily to preach against socialism. Once Alio decided Father Leo was the priest, there was only one thing left to do: shoot him.

During the 6 a.m. morning Mass on February 23, AD 1908, as the parishioners came to the altar rail to receive the Body, Blood, soul, and divinity of Jesus Christ in the Holy Eucharist, Giuseppe Alio also came forward. Each communicant received Our Lord upon the tongue. When Father Leo placed the Blessed Sacrament upon Alio's tongue, he spat the Sacred Host out of his mouth toward Father Leo, who was aghast at such an act of desecration. (Later, Alio claimed the Sacred Host "burned" his mouth.) As Father Leo started to bend over to recover the Sacred Host, Alio, only about a foot from the priest, brandished his revolver and with one shot pierced Father Leo's heart. The priest instantly lost his strength but managed to retrieve two Sacred Hosts that fell from the ciborium; Father Leo told the altar server to find Father Eusebius, ostensibly so he could recover the other Sacred Hosts that fell to the floor. The server found Father Wulstan and blurted out that Father Leo had been shot. When Father Wulstan got to Father Leo, the wounded priest had placed the ciborium upon the step of the altar dedicated to Our Lady. And there, still under the protective care of Our Lady, Father Leo, with a smile on his face, surrendered his life and his priesthood to the One who called him to model the priesthood of Jesus Christ in life and in death.

Alio tried to flee St. Elizabeth's church, but an alert off-duty police officer subdued the assailant until he could be carried away to police headquarters.

Four years after his burial, Father Leo's grave was opened in order to move it to another location. It was discovered that, although his habit had deteriorated, his body was in a remarkable state of preservation. His grave had already been, and continues to be, a place of pilgrimage. Miracles have been credited to his intercession. In AD 1938, the Archdiocese of Denver began the proceedings into the possible canonization of Father Leo Heinrichs, who died in the very act of sharing the Body of Jesus Christ with others.

Reflection

Father Leo died in the manner in which he lived his whole life: bringing Jesus Christ to others and bringing others to Jesus Christ. That is a priest's *raison d'etre*. A priest is a conduit of divine grace and a means by which a soul, starving for contact and communion with Christ Jesus, is brought to Him. When a priest gives someone Holy Communion, it is as if he places the pierced hand of Christ into the hand of the believer, which is similar to when a father gives his daughter away during the marriage ceremony. The priest is privileged to preside over the entire union between Christ and the believer as a spiritual father.

Father Leo fulfilled his priestly ministry in an exemplary and heroic manner. He literally died sharing Jesus Christ in the Blessed Sacrament with others. Father Leo's ordination was a reflection of God's design for his life. And his martyrdom while celebrating Holy Mass is God's acceptance of a priestly life lived in perfect conformity with the priesthood of Jesus Christ.

Though the baptized cannot mediate Christ in the same manner as an ordained priest, all the baptized do share in the universal priesthood of Jesus Christ. All the baptized are called to share the gift of Jesus Christ with others in their words and deeds. The witness of Father Leo reminds us that, as glorious as it is to die for Jesus, "red martyrdom" must be preceded by "white martyrdom." We must live every day to the best of our ability for Jesus. To apply the Great Doxology of the Eucharistic Prayer, we must live "through Him, and with Him, and in Him." That is the vocation of the baptized. That is the life that awaits us in Heaven.

Chapter 7
SAINT OSCAR ROMERO

Martyred March 24, AD 1980
San Salvador, El Salvador

IN the capital city of San Salvador, a single gunshot rang out Monday evening in the small hospital chapel known as the Chapel of Divine Providence. Archbishop Oscar Romero, sixty-two years of age, had just preached what would be his last homily. Standing at the altar for the beginning of the Liturgy of the Eucharist, he was struck in the chest by an assassin's bullet, instantly falling to the floor at the feet of the image of the Crucified Jesus who seemed to look to heaven supplicating the Father to accept the ultimate sacrifice of this archbishop's life.

For three years as Archbishop of San Salvador, and despite a failed assassination attempt the preceding month, Romero tirelessly and tenaciously preached the Gospel of Life; he defended the sanctity of all human life and the fundamental rights of the people against an oppressive and terrorizing government. In the estimation of many, his elevation from being the bishop of Santiago de Maria to the archbishop of San Salvador was questionable at best. He was perceived to be one who would respect the status quo with the government and would shy away from political confrontation by not meddling with official governmental policy and practices. In this respect, Oscar

Romero's appointment to be the archbishop of San Salvador paralleled another archbishop's appointment centuries earlier in England: St. Thomas a Becket, chosen by King Henry II; Thomas too was thought to be a "safe" appointment at least by those in the English government, but as history shows, Thomas was transformed by grace and would similarly lay down his life in protection of the people entrusted to his pastoral care.

There is something revelatory about Archbishop Romero's martyrdom. He died celebrating the "mystery of Faith" because he had first lived "the mystery of Faith" with integrity throughout his life. His death instantiates the mystery he faithfully celebrated. When a man is ordained to the sacred priesthood, the ordaining bishop addresses the priest: "[I]mitate the mystery you celebrate: model your life on the mystery of the Lord's cross."

"Imitate the mystery you celebrate." The "mystery celebrated" is the mystery of the Mass, and the mystery of the Mass is the mystery of Jesus's self-sacrificing love, a love that laid down His life for others. This is the connection between imitating the mystery celebrated and modeling one's life on the mystery of the Lord's cross. The Mass makes the historical event a present reality. From the theological perspective, there is actually only one Mass, with Jesus Himself as the sacrificing Priest and the Sacrifice offered; every Mass subsequently celebrated participates in that one Mass, one Priesthood, and one Sacrifice that is now for all ages.

As a priest and as a bishop, Oscar Romero's spiritual life fittingly centered on the Eucharist; this included the faithful celebration of the Eucharist as well as the regular adoration of Jesus in the Blessed Sacrament. (These two interrelated dimensions of this "mystery," that is, celebrating and adoring, flow out of and into one other.) He authentically lived what the Second Vatican Council declared: "The Eucharist is the source and summit of the Christian life."[6] From the countless hours he spent adoring Jesus really and truly present in the Blessed

6 *Catechism of the Catholic Church*, no. 1324, Quoting LG 11.

Sacrament and through his faith-filled celebration of the Eucharist, he was transformed into the mystery he adored and celebrated: the mystery of self-sacrificing love. The manner of his death is thus a fitting witness to the central role of the Eucharist and the relationship between ultimate love and ultimate sacrifice; true love cannot exist without sacrifice or self-donation. The power of the Eucharist, if a person enters into that mystery, will thoroughly transform him into this most sacred mystery. Archbishop Oscar Romero did.

Once Oscar Romero was made archbishop of San Salvador, he frequently visited the chapel of Divine Providence to make his holy hour. He needed this for himself to gain the strength and the grace to fulfill the demands of his office. Eucharistic adoration became the furnace by which his soul was enflamed to care for the sick and suffering, to visit the imprisoned, and to advocate for the poor and oppressed. Without the power of the Eucharist, Romero would have been impotent to fulfill his mandate from God to be the principal shepherd of the people of San Salvador. Sister Luz Isabel, the local superior of the sisters at the hospital, personally observed Archbishop Romero's piety and ardor during these Eucharistic visits.

Eucharistic adoration and the celebration of the Eucharist are not in competition, as some today suggest. Saint Oscar Romero's life bears witness that both expressions of Eucharistic piety, adoration and celebration, nurture each other.

Archbishop Oscar Romero was canonized by Pope Francis on October 14, AD 2018.

Reflection

Archbishop Romero's life demonstrates the moral imperatives of the Eucharist. To receive Jesus, Body, Blood, soul, and divinity, in the Holy Eucharist is never a solitary act with no moral mandate. Oftentimes, Christianity is presented as a "me and Jesus" affair. Jesus, however, feeds us with Himself precisely to reorient our myopic perspective; as descendants of Adam and Eve, we are inordinately attached to our own hopes and desires, oftentimes to the exclusion of others around us. The *Catechism of the Catholic Church* states bluntly: "To receive in truth the Body and Blood of Christ given up for us, we must recognize Christ in the poorest, his brethren."[7]

Because Archbishop Romero was thoroughly devoted to the Eucharist in adoration and in celebrating the Mass, his eyes were opened to the existential plight of those around him. Because the Eucharist was the personal source and summit of his life, he could recognize Jesus's hidden presence not only in the transubstantiated Bread and Wine but also His presence in the poor and the oppressed. Because the Eucharist is the mystery of self-sacrificing love, Archbishop Romero could not remain idle, sitting comfortably in his residence, doing nothing, saying nothing, observing the status quo. He acted; he spoke out; he defended the image of Jesus in those who could not defend themselves. Christian love, as the Eucharist communicates to us, is an active love, a love the seeks to make a positive difference, a love that reaches out to bring the presence of Christ to those who need Him most. Archbishop Romero knew that in receiving the Eucharist, we are never alone, and we can never isolate ourselves from His presence outside the Sacrament.

The Eucharist commits us to helping others, or else we eat and drink condemnation upon ourselves for failing to discern the Body of Jesus beyond His sacramental Presence (see 1 Cor 11:29). How has our Eucharistic reception changed us? Are we more attentive to the needs of others? Are we actively making a positive difference in the lives of others? Or do we receive the Eucharist with no thought about others? Saint Oscar Romero is a kind of patron saint for Eucharistic adoration and for fruitful Eucharistic reception. May he pray for us that we can see Jesus in whatever appearance He takes, in the Sacrament and in each other.

---

7 *Catechism of the Catholic Church*, no. 1397.

Chapter 8

Catholics in Iraq

Martyred August 1, AD 2004; October 31, AD 2010;
December 25, AD 2013
Baghdad and Mosul, Iraq

ABOUT one hundred twenty parishioners of the Syrian Catholic Church gathered for the vigil Mass of All Saints in Baghdad's church of Our Lady of Salvation on October 31, AD 2010. Six years earlier, on August 1, AD 2004, this same church, as well as five other Catholic churches in Baghdad and Mosul, was the scene of a terrorist attack as parishioners left Mass. Car bombs exploded, killing at least twelve people and wounding at least seventy-one others. They were killed for the simple reason that they were Catholics and attending Mass provided the terrorists with an opportunity to rid the areas of Mosul and Baghdad of "infidels."

As the parishioners at Our Lady of Salvation prepared for the Holy Sacrifice of the Mass on All Saints' Vigil, loud explosions rocked the church; gunfire quickly ensued. Almost immediately, gunmen, donned with suicide vests laced with ball bearings, burst into the church, locking the doors behind them and shouting such things as "infidels" and "you are all going to hell." The priest of the parish was in the sanctuary; grasping for a crucifix, he pleaded with the gunmen to spare his parishioners. They opened fire on him, killing him instantly. After killing the priest, the gunmen turned on the congregation and opened fire on the people. Dozens and dozens were killed. Not content with killing innocent human life, the gunmen spewed their hatred toward Catholicism by destroying sacred images, such as a crucifix and an image of the Blessed Virgin Mary.

After this initial attack, those who survived were herded into another room where they were held as hostages for approximately four hours. Many were physically attacked and beaten by the gunmen. The second priest was discovered; he had helped hide some families in the interior of the church when the assault began. As he confronted the gunmen, he implored them to stop the killing, he was promptly shot in the head. A mother pled for the life of her young son. The gunmen shot them both; the son died, but the mother survived the gunshot wound to her back. A young woman who walked to Mass that evening in order to tell the priest who recently married her that she was with child and would give birth in several months was murdered in the attack with her preborn child. One of the youngest victims was Adam Udai, a three-year-old precious child, who is reported to have said to the gunmen, "please stop," before being ruthlessly killed.

Reports are conflicting, but either one of the gunmen set off his suicide vest or he threw a grenade into the crowd. Whichever it was, the carnage continued. Survivors relate that "human flesh was everywhere." The Iraqi anti-terrorist unit, known as "the Golden Force," responded, and after a failed attempt to overpower the gunmen, eventually succeeded. By ten o'clock in the evening, the gunmen were killed in the liberation of the hostages, as were some of the parishioners, though exact numbers are not known. What is known is that fifty-eight people were martyred on October 31, AD 2010. Perhaps Sama Wadie, a thirty-two-year-old teacher and survivor, said it best: "This gives us more strength. We're not afraid of death because Jesus died for us. Of course, we cry, but they're tears of happiness, because we die for God."

Reflection

What if going to Mass meant one could be killed for that decision? Would we go? Such a scenario is hard to imagine in the United States, but that is the reality for many of our Catholic brothers and sisters living and practicing their faith in Iraq and in other parts of the world. On at least three different occasions (August 1, AD 2004; October 31, AD 2010; and December 25, AD 2013), Catholics were killed simply because they chose to go to Mass in Iraq; the threat of violence and death did not deter them from approaching Jesus, the Bread of Life. The words of Jesus, "He who eats my flesh and drinks my blood has eternal life, and I will raise him up at the last day" (Jn 6:54), were their motivation and their salvation.

We can lose sight of the spiritual reality of what the Mass is and who it is that we receive. There are men, women, and children who literally risk their lives to receive Our Lord in Holy Communion. How can we, who have no excuse, excuse ourselves from participating in the greatest act of worship possible, the self-offering of the Son to His Father in the power of the Holy Spirit? We need this communion with the Living God to free us from selfishness and to empower us to offer our lives as a sacrifice of love. The Eucharist is all about love, divine love. Jesus comes as love, and He comes in love to draw us into the communion of love that is God Himself.

This great Sacrament has the potential to transform us into a more perfect image of the One who is Love-in-the-flesh.

Chapter 9
Servant of God Jacques Hamel

Martyred July 26, AD 2016
Saint-Etienne-du-Rouvay, France

HE has been called "Europe's first martyr of the twenty-first century." Father Jacques Hamel, an eighty-five-year-old retired French diocesan priest, was viciously attacked and killed by two teenage Muslim extremists on July 26, AD 2016, while celebrating the Holy Sacrifice of the Mass.

The two youths burst into the church during the Prayer of the Faithful shouting, "Allahu Akbar," which is Arabic for "Allah is great!" Immediately they made their way to the sanctuary where Fr Hamel stood; in the tussle that ensued, Father Hamel was knocked to the ground. Witnesses report they heard Father Hamel shout twice, "Satan, be gone!" The attackers then slit Fr Hamel's throat; he died within minutes. As the attackers fled the church that they desecrated by this sacrilegious murder, police shot and killed them both.

As news spread of the murder of Father Hamel, cries of "Santo Subito" (sainthood quickly) were heard all over France and beyond. Even the secular press called Father Hamel a "martyr." Pope Francis waived the usual five-year "wait and see" period so that the cause for the canonization of Father Hamel could begin. With the approbation from the Congregation for the Causes of Saints, Father Hamel's cause could move forward. Consequently, Father Hamel received the title "Servant of God."

Martyrdom seemed "to stamp" itself indelibly into Jacques Hamel's life beginning with the day of his birth. He was born in AD 1930 on the feast of St. Andrew the Apostle (November 30), who was the brother of St. Peter and a martyr for the Gospel of Jesus Christ, being crucified on an X-shaped cross. Jacques was ordained a priest of Jesus Christ on June 30, AD 1958, on the day that became the feast of the first martyrs of Rome, a commemoration of hundreds, if not thousands, of men and women who were tortured and martyred under the Roman Emperor Nero. In terms of Father Hamel's spirituality, he had a strong devotion to, and affinity with, St. Charles de Foucauld, who was martyred in Algeria in AD 1916. Like Father Hamel, St. Charles was known by the people as one who loved to help those in need. St. Charles's martyrdom, like that of Father Hamel's, sent shock waves throughout the community. The question in people's hearts, both at the time of St. Charles's martyrdom and Father Hamel's martyrdom was the same: How could someone do this to one who did nothing but good?

Reflection

The witness of Father Jacques Hamel is a moving reminder to all Catholics that the age of martyrdom is not something relegated to the past. In fact, it is estimated that in the twentieth century alone, more men and women were martyred for their Catholic faith than in all previous centuries combined! That is a staggering statistic. And though only into the twenty-first century by a couple of decades, the rate of martyrdom is on track to equal, or perhaps even surpass, the martyrdoms of the twentieth century. For as long as the Church exists in the world, martyrdom will be a reality. Recall the words of

Jesus to His apostles during the Last Supper discourse: "If you were of the world, the world would love its own; but because you are not of the world, but I chose you out of the world, therefore the world hates you. Remember the word that I said to you: 'A servant is not greater than his master.' If they persecuted me, they will persecute you" (Jn 15:19–20). Jesus assures His followers though: "Blessed are those who are persecuted for righteousness' sake, for theirs is the kingdom of heaven" (Mt 5:10).

Martyrdom, for any aspect of the Catholic faith, but especially for that core belief that is the "source and summit" of our lives as Catholics, is both a tragedy and a blessing. It is a tragedy because of the pain and torture imposed on another human being, made in the image of God. But at the same time, martyrdom is a blessing for the entire Church and, indeed, the world. An act of martyrdom reminds us that there are some truths we dare not compromise; there are some truths worth dying for. In a world that is so easily swayed as to what is true, the martyr is a sentinel for objective truth and the sovereignty of almighty God.

Part Two

Those Martyred in Defense or Protection of the Most Blessed Sacrament

Chapter 1
Saint Tarcisius

Martyred AD 257
Rome, Italy

THE details of the story of St. Tarcisius are unfortunately shrouded in mystery and probably lost forever in the past. In some versions, Tarcisius was a young child, about twelve years old; in other versions he was a deacon. But regardless of those discrepancies, Tarcisius was an actual historical person who experienced martyrdom defending the Holy Eucharist. The broader facts may not be known with certainty, but his existence and the circumstances of his death are.

As attested by St. Justin the Martyr in his *First Apology*, the custom developed very early in the Church's devotional life of taking the Holy Eucharist to the faithful who could not be present for the communal celebration of the sacred liturgy.[8] Normally such a ministry was entrusted to deacons. Whether Tarcisius was a deacon or whether no deacons were available and Tarcisius was asked to help, he was given the tremendous blessing and responsibility of bringing

[8] See St. Justin Martyr, *First Apology* 67, accessed February 20, 2024, https://www.newadvent.org/fathers/0126.htm.

the Blessed Sacrament to fellow Catholics who had been arrested and put in prison.

Without having a record of the actual conversation between the priest and Tarcisius, we could imagine the dialogue. The priest no doubt cautioned Tarcisius to travel directly to those imprisoned, for he carried the Lord and Savior Himself. "Guard the Eucharist with your very life," was the charge Tarcisius was given, and one he accepted with the utmost seriousness and tender devotion.

Tarcisius probably carried the Holy Eucharist in a cloth that he held close to his body as he made his way through the streets to the prison. As Tarcisius traveled with the Blessed Sacrament pressed against his heart, he was intimately aware that Jesus Christ, the King of kings and the Lord of lords, the One who healed the blind and cured the leper, the One who suffered, died, and rose, was with him; he was a "Christ-bearer" at that moment. Tarcisius may have sung a hymn to his Lord, or prayed for those who would receive the Eucharist from his hands, or simply declared his love for Jesus with each step he took.

Consumed with the presence of the One who traveled with him, Tarcisius may have been oblivious to those along the way. And when he was seen preoccupied with something he carried close to his heart, this may only have piqued the curiosity of others. What was he in a hurry to do? What was so important that he could not take time to converse? What was that thing he pressed next to his heart?

Tarcisius was intercepted and stopped by others. They demanded to know what he was doing, and even more, to know what he carried. Tarcisius remembered the counsel that sent him on his mission: Guard the Eucharist with your very life. When Tarcisius did not reveal the Treasure he carried, the others physically assaulted him, punching him with their hands and kicking him once he fell to the ground. Some may have used clubs to beat him. They grabbed at his hands, trying to force him to release what he carried. No one, no matter the force used, could wrench his hands apart to retrieve it from him. He clutched the precious cloth and its sacred Content with such resolve and strength that no one prevailed upon him.

According to tradition, a praetorian, named Quadratus, who was Catholic, though a secret one, saw the confrontation and broke it up, but not before Tarcisius was mortally wounded. As Quadratus carried Tarcisius in his arms to take him to the priest, Tarcisius died of his wounds, still clutching the Eucharist next to his heart.

Pope Benedict XVI, in AD 2010, shared the story of Saint Tarcisius with hundreds of altar servers present in Rome for an audience. The Holy Father concluded his retelling of this beautiful story of faith in the Real Presence of Jesus in the Eucharist with these words: "The Most Blessed Sacrament was not found on St. Tarcisius' body, either in his hands or his clothing. It explains that the consecrated Host which the little Martyr had defended with his life, had become flesh of his flesh thereby forming, together with his body, a single immaculate Host offered to God."[9] Martyrdom is indeed a Eucharistic act.

Reflection

Those words of Pope Benedict XVI, that the flesh of Tarcisius and the flesh of the Eucharist had become one, remind us of what Jesus said of marriage: the two shall become one flesh. The Eucharist is the wedding feast of the Lamb of God. Through the gift of the Eucharist, our flesh and the flesh of Christ do become one, united in love, and we are filled with sanctifying grace. Through the Eucharist, we will be transformed more perfectly into the image and likeness of the One we receive.

Do I long for intimacy with Jesus? Do I want to be one with Him? Do I love what He loves? Do I want what He wants? Do I think what He thinks? Am I truly becoming one with Him in every

---

9 Pope Benedict XVI, General Audience (August 4, 2010), https://www.vatican.va/content/benedict-xvi/en/audiences/2010/documents/hf_ben-xvi_aud_20100804.html.

dimension of my being and personality? Does my reception of the Eucharist help me to live more authentically the Christ-life I was first given in Baptism?

Chapter 2
SAINT HERMENEGILD

Martyred April 13, AD 585
Seville, Spain

THE events that led to the martyrdom of Saint Hermenegild began almost 270 years before his martyrdom and on a different continent. A priest from Alexandria, Egypt, Arius, the son of Ammonius, taught that the Second Person of the Trinity was not co-eternal with God the Father. Arius summarized his view as follows: "there was a time that the Son was not."[10] Arius argued that the Father is superior to the Son in terms of nature and time, and therefore the Son is not divine and cannot licitly be called "God the Son." Arius, described by his contemporaries as tall, lean, ascetical in appearance, and possessing an intellectual superiority above most others, was ordained a priest in AD 313. Soon he attracted a following, and his doctrine came under increasing scrutiny.

It was not long before the priest was denounced by his own bishop as teaching a heretical view of the Son of God. He had many

---

[10] Translated by John Henry Newman and Archibald Robertson. From Nicene and Post-Nicene Fathers, Second Series, Vol. 4. Edited by Philip Schaff and Henry Wace. (Buffalo, NY: Christian Literature Publishing Co., 1892.) Revised and edited for New Advent by Kevin Knight. https://www.newadvent.org/fathers/28161.htm.

defenders, but many, too, rejected his Christological theory. The growing controversy, which seemed to disturb all of Christianity, and on which all Christians seemed to have an opinion, climaxed in the Church's first-ever ecumenical Council, the Council of Nicaea, convened in AD 325.

Though there were approximately eighteen hundred bishops in the East and West, all of whom were invited to participate in the Council, only about three hundred bishops made the journey to the large, prosperous city that was south of Constantinople. Arius attended in order to present and defend his doctrine. The Council lasted about a month and was predominated by the Arian controversy; in the end, when the Council Fathers (i.e., the attending bishops) debated and voted on Arius's doctrine, it was summarily dismissed as heretical, and it was decreed that the Second Person of the Trinity was "God from God, Light from Light, true God from true God, begotten, not made, consubstantial with the Father." This formula is a categorical repudiation of Arianism.

As historically and theologically significant as the first-ever ecumenical council was, it did not immediately eradicate the Arian heresy. In fact, the heresy, ensconced in certain locations throughout the empire, particularly among the Germanic tribes, lingered for centuries before its eventual demise.

One such group in which Arianism thrived was the Visigoths. In AD 568, the Arian Leovigild, father of St. Hermenegild, became king of the Visigoths in the area south of the Pyrenees Mountains that included most of modern-day Spain. Leovigild's two sons, Hermenegild and Recared, both of whom were Arians at this time, were given a share in their father's expanding kingdom.

As was the custom of the day, Leovigild arranged a marriage for his son Hermenegild. In AD 579, Hermenegild married Ingund, the daughter of King Sigebert I of Austrasia, which was in France. Ingund and her family were devout Catholics. Sometime into the marriage, Hermenegild chose to renounce Arianism and embrace the Catholic faith as expressed in the Nicene Creed. This profession of Catholic faith infuriated his father and put the two in direct, armed conflict. Hermenegild sought assistance from his father's political enemies. Eventually, however, Hermenegild was betrayed, and while he sought sanctuary in a church, his brother, Recared, at his father's bidding, lured him out under a false promise of clemency. Once Leovigild had Hermenegild in his camp, he ordered him to be bound in chains, stripped of the outward signs of his royal dignity and office, and imprisoned in a dark, dank dungeon in Seville in AD 585. Additionally, in a futile attempt to dissuade Hermenegild from his Catholic faith, his father personally commanded his son be repeatedly tortured.

Hermenegild not only accepted the cross of torture and imprisonment in reparation for his sins and for the conversion of his family and all the Visigoths, but he also added austerities to those his father imposed. His father repeatedly entreated his son to return to his senses and to return to Arianism, and in exchange, Leovigild would restore Hermenegild's royal dignity. Hermenegild is reported to have written to his father, "I confess your goodness to me has been extreme. I will preserve to my dying breath the respect, duty, and tenderness which I owe you; but is it possible that you should desire me to prefer worldly greatness to my salvation? I value the crown as nothing; I am ready to lose scepter and life too, rather than abandon the divine truth."[11]

On April 13, AD 585, an Arian bishop, at Leovigild's command, went to Hermenegild in prison with the promise of a complete pardon if he would now receive Holy Communion from him. Hermenegild knew that to receive Communion from a heretic implied he was in communion of mind and heart with the heresy. Hermenegild

---

11 Alban Butler, *The Lives of the Fathers, Martyrs, and Other Principal Saints*, vol. 4 (Dublin: James Duffy, 1866), accessed February 16, 2024, https://www.bartleby.com/lit-hub/lives-of-the-saints/volume-iv-april/st-hermenegild-martyr/.

was not and therefore could not betray his Catholic faith by a sacrilegious Communion.

Furthermore, Hermenegild knew that whatever the Arian bishop offered him could not be Communion in the Catholic sense. Holy Communion is the Body, Blood, soul, and *divinity* of Jesus Christ. Arians denied the divinity of Jesus, so how could they intend to transubstantiate the bread and wine into the Eucharist as Jesus and His Church taught? No, Hermenegild would not receive Communion, and no power on earth could coerce him to do so. Upon learning of Hermenegild's refusal to receive Communion from the Arian bishop, the enraged Leovigild dispatched soldiers to decapitate his son in the dungeon.

Soon after Hermenegild's martyrdom, Recared was inspired to embrace the Catholic faith. Through his example and the intercession of the martyr Hermenegild, the Visigoth people too returned to the apostolic Faith of the Catholic Church.

Reflection

Suppose we were imprisoned, our dignity and power stripped from us, and all it took to be liberated, to be restored to a position of prestige and comfort, was to say a few words with our mouths and receive a Communion we knew was not valid. Would we? Would we sacrifice our personal integrity for a few years of comfort?

This perennial challenge of integrity is played out in every generation, and every person of every generation must find a way to be true to what they know to be true. This was the real drama of the incredible play, *A Man For All Seasons*, by Robert Bolt. Once Thomas More had been imprisoned for failing to swear to the Oath of Succession, his daughter Margaret, whom he called "Meg," visited him in prison to convince him to swear to the oath but not to mean it in his heart, a situation similar to St. Hermenegild's plight. Here is the dialogue between St. Thomas More and his beloved daughter, Margaret, from *A Man For All Seasons*:

> Margaret "God more regards the thoughts of the heart than the words of the mouth." Well, so you've always told me.
>
> Thomas Yes.
>
> Margaret Then say the words of the oath and in your heart think otherwise.
>
> Thomas What is an oath then but words we say to God. Listen, Meg. When a man takes an oath, he's holding his own self in his own hands, like water. And if he opens his fingers then, he needn't hope to find himself again. Some men aren't capable of this, but I'd be loathed to think your father one of them.

Words have meaning, and our actions have consequences. St. Hermenegild died for integrity; he had to be true to God because he knew, before all else, that he was a disciple of Jesus Christ, true God and true man, who gave us Himself, Body, Blood, soul, and divinity, in the Sacrament of His Real Presence.

Could we, would we, endure hardship for the truth of Jesus and the truth of the Eucharist?

Chapter 3
The Gorkum Martyrs

Martyred July 9, AD 1572
Briel, the Netherlands

IN AD 1572, Father John, a Dominican originally from Germany but assigned to a parish in Horner in the Netherlands, could not believe what he heard: the priests in the neighboring town of Gorkum had been arrested and imprisoned by radical Calvinist pirates called "Sea Beggars." The Netherlands at this time in history was in the grip of intense religious and political conflict. Only a few years previously, the region found itself engulfed in what would become known as the "Eighty-Years War," also called the "Dutch Revolt," ending in 1648. The conflict was precipitated by the ardent desire to rid themselves of all things Spanish; their hatred concentrated on the Spanish religion, that is, Catholicism, and the Spanish government, specifically King Philip II of Spain.

Despite the danger to his own life, and the distinct possibility of his own capture, Father John immediately knew what he had to do: go to his brother priests and bring them the grace and consolation of the sacraments. Donning a disguise, Father John set out for Gorkum. He ministered clandestinely to the thirteen imprisoned priests and two imprisoned brothers, most of whom were Franciscans; he was also able to minister to frightened Catholics in Gorkum, including the celebration of at least one baptism of an infant. Within a few days, the inevitable happened, and Father John, together with three other priests, was discovered, arrested, and imprisoned with the others.

There were eleven Franciscans (nine priests and two brothers), four secular or diocesan priests, two Norbertine priests, one Augustinian canon, and one Dominican, Father John. All together, nineteen men were imprisoned simply for holding the Catholic faith and ministering to others in the name of Jesus Christ. Quickly their imprisonment turned from mere incarceration to torture with countless acts of indignities. Their captors took turns torturing the nineteen priests and religious. They were promised freedom if they renounced and abjured the doctrines of Transubstantiation and Papal Primacy. All nineteen heroically refused to do so. Instead, it elicited from them renewed acts of faith. Crowds gathered to see the spectacle of the tortured priests and brothers, as if they were animals on display in a zoo; for a fee, the people in the crowd were permitted to see the prisoners and jeer at them themselves.

The group was transferred from Gorkum to the adjacent city of Briel. During their transfer, the nineteen sang the *Te Deum*, thanking God that they had been judged worthy to suffer for the holy Catholic faith. They also sang the *Salve Regina* and the *Stabat Mater*, beseeching Our Lady for her powerful and maternal intercession. Again, their captors cajoled them to repudiate the doctrine of the Real Presence of Jesus in the Most Blessed Sacrament. And again, to a man, they refused. At this point, their fates were sealed: martyrdom was their destiny.

After torture and abuse, the nineteen were hanged to death on July 9, AD 1572, and their bodies, after death, were hacked to pieces and then summarily thrown into a nearby ditch.

The nineteen glorious martyrs of Gorkum are:

- Leonard van Veghel (born AD 1527), secular priest
- Peter of Assche (born AD 1530), Franciscan lay brother
- Andrew Wouters (born AD 1542), secular priest
- Nicasius of Heeze (born AD 1522), Franciscan friar
- Jerome of Weert (born AD 1522), Franciscan friar
- Anthony of Hoornaar (date of birth unknown), Franciscan friar
- Godfried van Duynen (born AD 1502), secular priest
- Willehad of Denemarken (born AD 1482), Franciscan friar
- James Lacobs (born AD 1541), Norbertine
- Francis of Roye (born AD 1549), Franciscan friar
- John of Cologne (born c. AD 1500–1510), Dominican friar
- Anthony of Weert (born AD 1523), Franciscan friar
- Theodore of der Eem (born c. AD 1500), Franciscan friar
- Cornelius of Wijk bij Duurstede (born AD 1548), Franciscan lay brother
- Adrian van Hilvarenbeek (born AD 1528), Norbertine
- Godfried of Mervel (born AD 1512), Franciscan friar
- Jan of Oisterwijk (born AD 1504), canon regular of St. Augustine
- Nicholas Poppel (born AD 1532), secular priest
- Nicholas Pieck (born AD 1534), Franciscan friar

Not long after their martyrdom, pilgrimages began to visit the place of their martyrdom and their graves. Reports of miracles abounded. There is even a story that a beautiful bush bearing nineteen exquisite white flowers grew on the spot of their martyrdom.

The nineteen holy martyrs of Gorkum were beatified November 14, AD 1675, by Pope Clement X, and they were canonized on June 29, AD 1867, by Pope Blessed Pius IX.

Reflection

The Catholic Church defines a martyr as someone who was put to death "*in odium fidei*." That is the Latin expression for "in hatred for the Faith." The nineteen Martyrs of Gorkum were martyrs for no other reason than because they were Catholic and specifically because they would not repudiate their Catholic faith in the Real Presence of Jesus in the Most Blessed Sacrament or in the pope's authority. Though given ample opportunities to go free, if they but renounced the core tenets of the Catholic faith, they did not. How easy it would have been for these nineteen men to rationalize and compromise. Though we do not have reports that these men had an interior debate about "the good" that would result if they did compromise their faith, the Enemy, Satan himself, quite likely tempted them to do so. Satan may well have presented them with thoughts such as these: "You can do more good if you compromise your faith now and live to help others." "Surely, God would understand if you momentarily deny the Real Presence amid such torture; He is merciful after all." "What good will come from your deaths? The dead can do nothing." "God doesn't really want you to suffer and die, but to live."

The concept of "compromise" is a valued political strategy; one could argue that the United States was founded on this concept. And politically there may be merit to this practice, under certain circumstances. But the concept does not translate into anything comparable with our Faith. We cannot compromise without losing our salvation and our very identity. As the great Southern writer, Flannery O'Connor, once wrote: "You don't join the Catholic Church. You become Catholic."[12] It is a mode of being and not something extrinsic to our identity. The one baptized into Christ Jesus is a "marked" person, indelibly marked, forever changed at the level of being. Our faith in Jesus Christ and in His Church defines who we are.

---

[12] Letter to Roslyn Barnes, December 12, 1960, in *The Habit of Being*, ed. Sally Fitzgerald (New York: Farrar, Straus and Giroux, 1979), 422.

Chapter 4
Blessed George Napier (also Napper)

Martyred November 9, AD 1610
Oxford, England

BLESSED George Napier was born around AD 1550 in the city of Oxford, England, the very city in which he would die as a martyr about sixty years later in AD 1610.

When George was eight years old, in AD 1558, Parliament, at the instigation of Queen Elizabeth I, enacted a new Act of Supremacy; this new act replaced the original Act of Supremacy of King Henry VIII of AD 1534. The new version contained a significant modification from the 1534 Act. In Henry's Act, he was declared "supreme head of the Church in England." The Act of 1558 replaced that title with "supreme governor of the Church in England." This revision was considered by many, but not by all, to be a softening of the Act of 1534 and a slight "nod" to Catholics who might find the new title a bit more palatable.

In AD 1566, George entered the prestigious Corpus Christi College in Oxford; two years later, however, he was expelled, not for academic reasons, but for the sole fact he was a "recusant," that is, a practicing Catholic who refused to attend the Anglican liturgy. If found guilty, the accused was subject to fines and/or imprisonment. The resolution of this charge against George Napier is not known with certainty. He does not appear to have been imprisoned at this time but in all likelihood was forced to pay a fine.

Things changed, though, in AD 1580, when George was arrested and imprisoned in a small jail in London. He was detained there until, in AD 1589, he accepted the revised Act of Supremacy of 1558, whereupon he was released.

George pursued ordination to the Catholic priesthood in the English College, located in Douai, France, and was ordained in AD 1596. After his ordination, Father George returned to England for the purpose of ministering to Catholics who were compelled to practice their faith in secret.

On Monday, July 19, AD 1610, Father George was apprehended by local authorities on the suspicion he was ministering as a Catholic priest. As proof of his illegal activities, he was searched, and found on his person were his breviary, oil stocks, and, most egregious of all, a pyx containing two consecrated Hosts. The possession of the Blessed Sacrament by Father George infuriated the authorities and guaranteed his arrest and possible execution. No other aspect of Catholicism, save affirming the supremacy of the Bishop of Rome, elicited as much vitriol as did the Catholic Church's affirmation of the Real and substantial Presence of Jesus in the Most Blessed Sacrament. According to the Thirty-Nine Articles, promulgated in AD 1571 as the defining articulation of the Anglican faith, the doctrine of Transubstantiation, which affirms that the substance of bread and wine are wholly and completely converted into the substance of the Body and Blood of Jesus Christ, is "repugnant to the plain words of Scripture." The Thirty-Nine Articles categorically rejected the doctrine of any change of substance in the Eucharistic elements. Instead, communicants receive a presence of Christ through their subjective faith.

Father George was placed in custody and brought before a justice in order to confirm their suspicion that he was a priest and thereby throw him into prison. The justice had him searched again, whereupon the breviary and the oil stocks were discovered, thus corroborating the testimony of the arresting official. But the most damaging, conclusive, and irrefutable evidence of his priesthood had "disappeared." The pyx with the two consecrated Hosts had vanished! When queried concerning its whereabouts, Father George remained silent.

Between the time of his arrest and his appearance before the justice, in all likelihood, Father George prayed in his heart that the Blessed Sacrament would be kept safe and preserved from the inevitable profanation that would have resulted upon its confiscation. Apparently, God heard the prayer of this holy priest and took to Himself the sacred and Eucharistic Body of His only begotten Son, preventing its sacrilegious treatment.

Even without the key evidence, Father George was nevertheless found guilty of being a priest and ministering to Catholics in England. This was a violation of the Jesuit, etc., Act of 1584. For this, he was condemned, but many believed he would eventually be released after several months of imprisonment. However, this all changed when, in November, AD 1610, it was discovered that Father George continued his priestly ministry even in jail as he reconciled to the Church a felon, a lapsed Catholic, condemned to die. Immediately, a sentence of death by being hanged, drawn, and quartered was imposed on Father George, and thus he died a martyr's death on November 9, AD 1610.

He was beatified by Pope Pius XI in AD 1929.

Reflection

The Thirty-Nine Articles of 1537 stated that the doctrine of Transubstantiation is "repugnant to the plain words of Scripture."[13] Is

13 Article 28, accessed February 20, 2024, http://anglicansonline.org/basics/thirty-nine_articles.html.

that really the case? What are the "plain words of Scripture" on the Eucharist? Jesus said, "This is my body" (Mt 26:26). (He did not say "this represents my body.") "This is my blood" (Mt 26:28). (He did not say "this is a symbol of my blood.") "My flesh is food indeed, and my blood is drink indeed" (Jn 6:56). (He did not say "my flesh is a metaphor for food.") "Unless you eat the flesh of the Son of man and drink his blood, you have no life in you" (Jn 6:53). The Greek verb for "eat" means "to munch, to gnaw." As His listeners began to reject His teaching, Jesus switches from using the usual Greek word for eating to a much more graphic verb, thus emphasizing the reality of His teaching. The "plain words of Scripture" do indeed reveal Jesus's true and real presence in the Eucharist.

St. Cyril of Jerusalem, a bishop who lived from AD 313 to AD 386, wrote a series of catechetical lectures for neophytes. In his Jerusalem Catecheses, he wrote: "Since then He Himself declared and said of the Bread, This is My Body, who shall dare to doubt any longer? And since He has Himself affirmed and said, This is My Blood, who shall ever hesitate, saying, that it is not His blood?"[14]

Jesus is not only a man of His word but He is the Word made flesh. In Genesis, when the Word declared, "let there be light," there was light. As the Word Incarnate, what He declares becomes reality. His words concerning the Eucharist are clear; His meaning is "plain." He is really and truly present. This was the faith of the Apostles; this was the faith of Blessed George Napier; this is our faith in the Word made flesh in the Eucharist.

---

[14] Translated by Edwin Hamilton Gifford. From *Nicene and Post-Nicene Fathers*, Second Series, Vol. 7. Edited by Philip Schaff and Henry Wace. (Buffalo, NY: Christian Literature Publishing Co., 1894.) Revised and edited for New Advent by Kevin Knight. https://www.newadvent.org/fathers/310122.htm.

Chapter 5
MANUEL

Martyred c. AD 1700
Vicinity of Jacksonville, Florida

THE fifteen-year-old Manuel was excited to hear the news from the priest in charge of Our Lady of Candelaria chapel: "Manuel, I have great news! I am recommending you to the seminary to study for the sacred priesthood!" He would be the first indigenous boy to enter the seminary in St. Augustine, Florida, and, if God so willed, the first indigenous Franciscan priest in the new world.

Manuel could hardly contain his joy. He ran home to tell his parents. They too were excited beyond words. Manuel's parents were converts to the Catholic faith, and they raised their son Manuel as a devout Catholic. As a youngster, Manuel began serving the Holy Mass at the chapel. As he matured and showed clear signs of a religious vocation, the priest asked Manuel to be the sacristan at Our Lady of Candelaria chapel. Without hesitation, he said, "Yes!"

A sacristan had many responsibilities, especially since the priest was not always available to oversee the sundry tasks required for the upkeep of the chapel. It was the sacristan's responsibility to keep the chapel, the vestments, and the vessels clean and prepared for divine worship. Above all, should the chapel be attacked or endangered in some way, the sacristan was to protect the Blessed Sacrament from desecration. Manuel accepted these responsibilities as an expression of his love for his faith and especially his love for Jesus in the Blessed Sacrament.

And then one day, the unthinkable happened: the village was attacked by the British and the Creek Indians. Their standard operating procedure was to attack the chapel first; this strategy was intended to draw out the priest and the Apalachee Indian chief so that they could be tortured in front of the tribe. They set the chapel on fire. Manuel ran to the blazing chapel, entered it, and frantically tried to extinguish the fire but to no avail. It had quickly spread and would soon devour everything. Manuel screamed, "Bring water quickly! Jesus is about to be burned!" He repeated his plea, but no one responded.

A British soldier and two Creek Indians watched Manuel as he desperately tried to save the chapel and the Blessed Sacrament. They taunted him for his efforts and advised him that, should he pray for water, that God would intervene. So, Manuel fell to his knees, and with arms outstretched, he prayed fervently for a miracle. His audience of three sneered and laughed at him and, with diabolical fury, hacked the arms off of the praying Manuel at his elbows. He was struck in the face with such force that he lost many of his teeth and his jaw was broken. The three dragged Manuel outside and forced him to watch as the tabernacle and the chapel were consumed by the fire.

Manuel was already close to death from their vicious attack, but the Creeks had one more assault, the *coup-de-grace*: they drowned him in the water trough for the horses.

The martyrdom of Manuel was witnessed by two Apalachee Indians who hid in the surrounding bushes; they gave sworn testimony to a notary in St. Augustine about the heroism and the gruesome martyrdom of the fifteen-year-old sacristan. Additionally, the British soldier who took part in Manuel's martyrdom was wounded upon leaving the village and was left for dead. Spanish soldiers who responded to the news of the British attack discovered the soldier and brought him to St. Augustine to receive medical treatment. After four months of recuperation, the British soldier gave testimony as to Manuel's martyrdom. His account of the events perfectly corresponded with the earlier report of the two Indians.

Manuel is being considered for beatification along with hundreds of others among the martyrs of La Florida.

Reflection

In Isaiah 11:6, there is a prophecy about the coming Messiah in the words, "and a little child shall lead them." These words could easily be appropriated and applied to Manuel. Though only fifteen years old, he leads us into a deeper appreciation for the greatest gift God could give us: the Gift of Jesus in the Blessed Sacrament. St. John Vianney once said, "There is nothing so great as the Eucharist. If God had something more precious, He would have given it to us." Manuel knew this, and his life and death bore witness to the centrality of the Eucharist in the life of the faithful.

Manuel, though a "little child" in the eyes of the world, who never wrote one word of theology, wrote a most elegant treatise in defense of the Real Presence with his life and death. He died for Jesus because he lived for Jesus; he died for Jesus because he loved Jesus in the Blessed Sacrament. That was his life, and now it is his eternity.

Can we say the same? What "story" do our lives communicate to others? Can others read our lives and there discover the centrality of the Blessed Sacrament?

Chapter 6

Blessed Simon Cardon and Companions (Martyrs of Casamari)

Martyred May 13–16, AD 1799
Lazio, Italy

FLANNERY O'Connor, the great southern, Catholic writer, once wrote to a friend on December 16, AD 1955: "I realize now that [the Eucharist] is the center of existence for me; all the rest of life is expendable."[15] Those words are perfectly realized in the martyrdom of six men who died in the Italian Abbey of Casamari at the hands of French Jacobin soldiers. The incredible story of the martyrs is not well-known in the English-speaking world, and that is a shame because the witness of these six men speaks volumes about the meaning of life and death, about what is most important in life, and that for which we should be willing to lay down our very lives. These men did that and, in so doing, they proclaimed in their blood the existential centrality of the Most Holy Eucharist. They forfeited their earthly life for a life of endless joy and happiness precisely because "all the rest of life is expendable."

[15] Letter to "A," December 16, 1955, in *The Habit of Being*, ed. Sally Fitzgerald (New York: Farrar, Straus and Giroux, 1979), 125.

On the evening of May 12, AD 1799, the Cistercian monks were preparing to pray Compline, the night prayer of the Church, when about fifteen French Jacobin soldiers presented themselves, asking to be fed. The community, in typical Benedictine tradition, extended hospitality to these men. After being fed, the soldiers turned hostile and demanded whatever treasure the Abbey housed. Father Simon Cardon, the claustral prior of Casamari Abbey, explained there was very little of value; he made no attempt to stop the soldiers as they ransacked the buildings in their search for valuables. Many of the monks, including the abbot, feared for their lives and fled the abbey, hiding in the adjacent fields. Six monks remained, perhaps with a premonition that the Real Treasure of the Abbey, Jesus Christ Himself, present in the Most Blessed Sacrament, would soon be the object of the soldiers' fury.

As feared, the soldiers moved from searching the Abbey buildings to ransacking the church, feverishly looking for some hidden treasure. As their search yielded nothing, the soldiers vented their anger by sacrilegiously destroying the tabernacle, that hallowed receptacle that contained the greatest of all Treasures: the Blessed Sacrament. For Father Simon and the five others of his community that remained, this was too far. They could have whatever earthly treasure they discovered in the abbey buildings, but an attack on the Blessed Sacrament was intolerable. The soldiers broke open the tabernacle and threw the ciborium containing the consecrated Hosts to the ground. The monks, who by virtue of staying behind made themselves "sentinels of the Blessed Sacrament," began methodically recovering the desecrated Hosts, but as they did so, the soldiers hunted them down like prey and, with swords drawn, slew the monks one by one.

The six Cistercian monks martyred for protecting the Blessed Sacrament were:

- Father Simon Cardon
- Father Domenico Maria Zawrel
- Brother Mathurin Marie Pitri
- Brother Modeste Marie Burgen
- Brother Albertino Marie Maisonade
- Brother Zosimo Maria Brambat

Shortly after their brutal martyrdom, the monks of Casamari buried their brothers in the community cemetery. As word spread of the heroic witness of the martyrs, the faithful flocked to pray at their graves. Miracles soon occurred in great numbers; the Lord wished to validate their ultimate testimony to the Real Presence of Jesus in the Blessed Sacrament. The otherwise tranquil surroundings of the abbey became excessively chaotic due to the influx of pilgrims seeking the heavenly help of the holy martyrs. To remedy the frenetic situation and to restore a semblance of peace and order for the monks, the abbot, in AD 1854, commanded, under holy obedience, that the martyrs cease answering the prayers and petitions of the pilgrims. A few years after the abbatial prohibition, the community transferred the bodies of the martyrs from the community cemetery to the abbey church. At that point the abbot lifted his command, and immediately the miracles resumed with even greater frequency than before.

The Martyrs of Casamari were beatified on April 17, AD 2021.

Reflection

In the Fourth Eucharistic Prayer of the Roman Missal, following the Consecration, the priest offers this prayer: "Look, O Lord, upon the Sacrifice which You Yourself have provided for Your Church, and grant in Your loving kindness to all who partake of this one Bread and one Chalice that, gathered into one body by the Holy Spirit, they may truly become a living sacrifice in Christ to the praise of Your glory."[16]

The theology of the prayer reflects what Baptism in Christ commits us to embrace: that our entire lives become a living sacrifice in Christ to the praise of God's glory; this is not automatic though; it must be intentional. Christ offered Himself in His humanity to the Father through the Holy Spirit not only in atonement for our sins but also as an act of sacrificial worship to the Father. He did this, not to alleviate us of the obligation to do likewise, but to empower and elevate our self-offering into His Self-offering. We exercise our baptismal priesthood by surrendering our bodies and souls to the Living God as an act of sacrificial worship.

God calls the martyrs of any age to remind all of us of the need to worship Him through the sacrifice of our lives. The martyrs, those who literally offered themselves, body and soul, as a sacrifice of praise to the One who poured out all He is to the Father in sacrificial worship, remind us in the most graphic manner of the debt of worship we owe the God who loved us into existence.

Do we approach the Holy Sacrifice of the Mass as the privileged place where we can unite ourselves to the once-in-time-sacrifice of the Son as an act of our worship in the here and now? Do we appreciate the Sacrifice of the Mass as the "power source" to live "eucharistically," that is, surrendering all we are, body and soul? Surrendering to Him all our cares and concerns, all our hopes and desires, our love?

---

[16] Catholic Church, *The Roman Missal* (Totowa, NJ: Catholic Book Publishing, 2011), 512.

Chapter 7

Saint Cesidio Giacomantonio, OFM

Martyred July 4, AD 1900
Hengyang, China

ANGELO Giacomantonio was born August 30, AD 1873, in Fossa, Italy, a town about eighty miles northeast of Rome. As an adolescent, Angelo frequented the Franciscan monastery of St. Angelo and eventually discerned a vocation to the order. He entered the postulancy when he was about seventeen years old. When Angelo began the novitiate, he received the Franciscan habit and his religious name: Cesidio. Cesidio was ordained to the sacred priesthood in AD 1897. The following year, he began preparation to become a missionary, and his superior encouraged Father Cesidio to ask to be sent to the mission in China. In October, AD 1899, he embarked for Hengyang, China, and arrived two months later on Christmas Day.

Simultaneously with Father Cesidio's departure for China, the Boxer Rebellion in China commenced. Fueling the Rebellion was xenophobia; it caused a kind of madness that gripped the country. Christianity, the missionaries, and indigenous converts, in particular, were especially targeted by the rebels as members and promoters of “the foreigners’ religion.” All thc ills within the country were blamed on foreigners and Christianity. Christianity was seen as a direct assault of the traditions of the people and an enemy to their received way of life. Merciless fury was vented upon Christians. It is estimated that thirty thousand Chinese Christian converts and missionaries were killed for their faith during this rebellion.

Father Cesidio had barely settled into his new home, when, on July 4, AD 1900, the rebels, in a surprise attack, descended on Hengyang and began killing Christians. Once he realized what was happening, Father Cesidio ran from the residence to the chapel: his only concern was to protect the Blessed Sacrament from profanation. Before Father Cesidio could reach the chapel, however, he was attacked, beaten, speared, wrapped in a gas-soaked blanket, and then set ablaze. Father Cesidio gave his life to protect the Lord Jesus Christ in the Blessed Sacrament. The words of His Lord and Master are fittingly applied to him: “Greater love has no man than this, that a man lay down his life for his friends” (Jn 15:13).

Father Cesidio was canonized by Pope St. John Paul II on October 1, AD 2000, together with 119 other Chinese martyrs.

Reflection

Saint Cesidio was indeed set ablaze by the rebels and burned to death, but before he was burned with gasoline, he was set ablaze with the fire of divine love of Jesus Christ. His martyrdom, as horrific and unimaginable as it was to be burned alive, can be seen as an expression of the divine love poured into the soul of Saint Cesidio in his baptism, a love intensified by the sacraments, especially the sacrament of divine love, the Most Holy Eucharist. Saint Cesidio’s martyrdom thus reminds all of us that we too must let the fire of divine love purify us and transform us into living likenesses of Jesus Christ. As the Holy Spirit descended upon Our Lady and the Apostles as "tongues of fire" (see Acts 2:3), we too are set ablaze to burn with divine love and to sacrifice our lives as a holocaust of love.

St. John of the Cross once compared the interior life of divine love in a person's soul to throwing a piece of wood into a fire.[17] At first, the wood pops and crackles, as the impurities of the wood are consumed by the fire. Soon, however, the wood is so penetrated by the fire that one cannot tell the difference between the wood and the fire. God's love is shared with us so that, like that piece of wood, we will be so penetrated with divine love that we effectively become one with the Living God.

St John Vianney, the patron saint for diocesan priests, wrote: "Every Consecrated Host is made to burn Itself up with love in a human heart."[18] Do we want to grow in love? Is the fire of divine love in our souls beginning to diminish due to our nonresponsiveness or our lukewarm disposition? Then cultivate one's devotion to the Most Blessed Sacrament. As we commune with the One who is Love-in-the-flesh, then the fire of divine love in our souls will be stoked.

---

17 John of the Cross, Living Flame of Love, prologue, 3, referenced in Luis Martinez, *The Sanctifier* (Daughters of St. Paul, 1982), 76.

18 Quote commonly ascribed to St. John Vianney. No source.

Chapter 8
Saint Pedro Maldonado

Martyred February 11, AD 1937
Chihuahua City, Mexico

THOUGH the Cristero War, a conflict opposing the anticlerical and anti-Catholic laws of the 1917 Mexican Constitution, formally ended in AD 1929, there were lingering effects of the persecution throughout different parts of Mexico. Father Pedro Maldonado, martyred in AD 1937 in northern Mexico, was a victim of these lingering effects of persecution.

Born on June 15, AD 1892, in Chihuahua, Pedro entered the diocesan seminary at age seventeen. He was known for his Eucharistic devotion, a characteristic that would define his life and death as a priest. "I have thought of always having my heart in heaven and in the tabernacle," said Pedro Maldonado to the rector of the seminary, another reflection of his Eucharistic faith.[19] For Pedro, glimpses of heaven could be found here on earth, in the tabernacle, in the Blessed Sacrament, since in heaven, souls are perfectly united to the Lord Jesus; this union is the very purpose and goal of His Eucharistic Presence. The Eucharist is an invitation to divine intimacy.

---

[19] Catholic Diocese of El Paso (website), "San Pedro De Jesus Maldonado," accessed February 19, 2024, https://www.elpasodiocese.org/san-pedro-de-jesus-maldonado.html.

Due to an escalation in religious persecution, many of the seminarians fled across the border to El Paso, Texas, to complete their theological studies. Pedro eventually did the same and was ordained to the sacred priesthood in the El Paso cathedral on January 25, AD 1918. He returned to Mexico to celebrate his first Solemn High Mass on the feast of Our Lady of Lourdes, to whom he always had a special devotion, on February 11, AD 1918.

Thus, Father Pedro began his ministry as a priest. He was especially devoted to the poor, assisting them with food, money, and clothing; he also had a passion for the religious education of the youth and adults.

Father Pedro would visit with the farmers at harvest time and bless the crops, asking the Lord to pour forth His blessing on the work of their hands. On more than one occasion, locusts invaded the fields, and the farmers besought Father Pedro to pray for the protection of their crops. Father Pedro prayed, and the locusts were driven away, sparing the produce from any damage.

Throughout his entire eighteen-year priesthood, Father Pedro was the subject of multiple persecutions. On Ash Wednesday, February 10, AD 1937, Father Pedro was betrayed by an acquaintance and apprehended by government soldiers. He was able to put two consecrated Hosts into his pyx and asked the Lord that he be permitted the grace to receive Him in Holy Communion at the moment of death. The soldiers beat Father Pedro with the butt of their rifles; they spat on him and dragged him to the town hall. They continued the brutal and merciless beatings; his skull was fractured and even an eye was dislodged; he lay on the floor covered in his own blood. With one of the last blows he received, the pyx was knocked out of his grasp, and the two consecrated Hosts were revealed. A soldier, recognizing the consecrated Hosts, picked them up and shoved them in Father Pedro's mouth with utter contempt for the Blessed Sacrament, saying, "Eat this! It's your last Communion!" And so, at the hands of a fallen-away Catholic, Father Pedro received his last

Holy Communion, thus being united to the Lord Jesus Christ in life and in death.

Father Pedro died the following day, February 11, AD 1937, the anniversary of his first Solemn Mass.

Father Pedro Maldonado was canonized by Pope St. John Paul II on May 25, AD 2000.

Reflection

Viaticum is "food for the journey." It is a person's last Communion as he prepares for the final "passing over" from this life to the life prepared for us by Jesus (see Jn 14:2–3). The *Catechism of the Catholic Church* states about viaticum: "As the sacrament of Christ's Passover, the Eucharist should always be the last sacrament of the earthly journey, the 'viaticum' for 'passing over' to eternal life. . . . It is the seed of eternal life and the power of resurrection, according to the words of the Lord: 'He who eats my flesh and drinks my blood has eternal life, and I will raise him up at the last day.'"[20]

Often viaticum as a person's final sacrament is neglected among the faithful. But there is no better preparation to be united with Jesus for all eternity than to be united with Him sacramentally in this life. Saint Pedro Maldonado knew the spiritual import of a "last Communion" and he asked the Lord expressly for this grace. This, too, should be a desire of all the faithful and a grace to be sought.

---

20 *Cathechism of the Catholic Church*, nos. 1517, 1524.

Chapter 9
"LI"

Martyred c. AD 1900 or c. AD 1949
China

SADLY, the details surrounding the Eucharistic martyrdom of this heroic young Chinese girl are shrouded in mystery and probably undiscoverable at this point. Not even her name is known, though, in some versions of this story, she is given the name Li, not as a matter of fact but as a matter of convenience in referring to her. She was apparently ten or eleven years old. Not even the date of her martyrdom is known, but most believe it probably occurred during the persecution of Catholics under the Communist reign in China, circa AD 1949. Some, however, believe it occurred during the Boxer Rebellion, placing her death around AD 1900.

Her story, as rendered in this account, will follow the version attributed to Archbishop Fulton J. Sheen, whose cause for canonization is pending. But his version presents some difficulties itself. This rendition for *Martyrs of the Eucharist* will not attempt to resolve the internal difficulties in Archbishop Sheen's account, nor tackle the variant accounts from others, but will focus on what seems most accepted as the actual events.

A couple of months before he died, Archbishop Sheen was interviewed on television. He was asked: "You have inspired millions of people all over the world. Who inspired you? Was it a pope?"[21] He responded it was not a pope, cardinal, another bishop, or even a priest or nun, but rather an eleven-year-old Chinese girl.

He explained that when the Communists took over China, they imprisoned a priest in the rectory near the church. After being locked up in the rectory, the priest looked out the window and was horrified to see the Communists enter the church. Once inside, they broke open the tabernacle and, in an act of desecration, threw the ciborium down, scattering the Hosts on the floor. The priest knew exactly how many Hosts had been in the ciborium: thirty-two.

When the Communists left, they either did not notice, or did not pay any attention to a young girl praying in the back of the church. That night, she returned and, slipping past the guard at the rectory, entered the church where she made a holy hour, probably in reparation for the desecration of the Blessed Sacrament perpetrated by the soldiers.

After her holy hour, she went into the sanctuary, knelt down, then bent over and received Jesus in Holy Communion off the floor with her tongue.

Each night, the girl returned to make her holy hour and receive Jesus in Holy Communion. On the thirty-second night, after having consumed the last Host, she accidentally made a noise that awoke the guard, who was asleep at his post by the priest's residence. From his bedroom window, the priest could only watch in horror as the heartrending scene unfolded before his eyes. The girl tried to run away, but the guard caught up with her and beat her to death with the butt of his rifle.

---

21 Fulton J. Sheen, *Treasure in Clay* (Doubleday: New York, NY, 1980). This quote also appears in various articles on the subject, including: "How a young Chinese girl inspired Archbishop Fulton Sheen to make a Holy Hour every day." Signs & Wonders, June 9, 2015. https://sign.org/articles/how-a-young-chinese-girl-80065.

Reflection

Though this young Chinese girl is nameless to us, Jesus knows her and no doubt called her by name on that fateful night to be with Him forever in heaven. Jesus promises in John 6 that those who eat His flesh will live forever. The witness of this young girl serves as a powerful testimony of the devotion we should have when receiving Jesus in Holy Communion.

Could I go into a church to receive Communion in which death was a real possibility? Do I believe this strongly? Am I willing to put my faith into practice by spending time in adoration of the Blessed Sacrament? If He is really there, then there is where I need to be.

Chapter 10

Blessed Janos (Anastasius) Brenner, OCist

Martyred December 15, AD 1957
Szentgotthard, Vas, Hungary

"I AM not afraid," Father Anastasius told the bishop who offered to reassign the young priest in light of threats made against him by the government. "I am happy to remain here." Father Anastasius, whose religious name means "Resurrection," was assigned as a chaplain to a parish with a school, and he proved to be extremely popular, particularly with the young people; his popularity caused many in the local Communist government to be suspicious of him and even jealous. They feared he would undermine their efforts to indoctrinate the young people with atheism.

Father Anastasius, in this regard, was a Hungarian version of a slightly older Polish priest, Father Karol Wojtyla, the future Pope John Paul II, who also incurred the ire of governmental officials for his popularity with young people. Like Father Wojtyla, Father Anastasius's message to the young people was one of hope and dignity: hope that in Christ Jesus our sufferings have meaning and even power; and dignity that comes from being made in the image of God, and no one and no government can take away this dignity.

For Father Anastasius, God was real, and he knew God personally and loved Him with all his heart, soul, mind, and strength. Anyone familiar with Father Anastasius could see his faith in and love for God; it was real and contagious. He inspired others by his witness to love God and serve Him. Holiness and truth are attractive qualities, and Father Anastasius embodied both. When those in the atheistic government learned this about Father Anastasius, someone made the decision that this priest was dangerous and had to be eliminated. Plans were quickly developed to address and remedy the problem of Father Anastasius.

On the night of December 14, AD 1957, just two years into his priestly ministry, Father Anastasius heard a knock on the rectory door. Upon opening the door, a young man, described as about seventeen years old and an altar server in the parish, stated his uncle was dying and was requesting Last Rites (with the Apostolic Pardon), along with Confession and Viaticum. Without hesitation, Father Anastasius went to the church in order to get the Blessed Sacrament, which would be the dying man's viaticum. He and the young man set out to his uncle's home.

Shortly before reaching the house, Father Anastasius was ambushed by several men and brutally attacked. He was stabbed thirty-two times; his bloodied body collapsed and fell to the ground, where the assailants continued their attack by crushing several bones in his neck; they stood on his neck, wishing to humiliate him as much as possible. His body was discovered the next morning. In his hands was the pyx, containing the Blessed Sacrament. As fierce as the attack against the body of the priest was, they could not touch the Body of the Lord because of the heroism of Father Anastasius. Father Anastasius defended the Blessed Sacrament from profanation with his very life. When this was learned, many began calling Father Anastasius "the Hungarian Tarsicius."

Those that perpetrated this heinous and sacrilegious murder did so to discourage others from embracing the Gospel as proclaimed by the witness of Father Anastasius. Far from having its desired effects, Father Anastasius was instantly hailed as a martyr, and his message was proclaimed louder in his death than in life. A chapel was built on the spot of Father Anastasius's martyrdom. Through his martyrdom, he rose, as his religious name foreshadowed, victorious in the life of the people of Hungary and beyond.

Father Janos Anastasius Brenner was beatified as a martyr on May 1, AD 2018.

Reflection

The Eucharist is the Sacrament of the Paschal Mystery; it instantiates not only the sacrifice of Christ, but His triumph as well—His resurrection. Jesus promised that those who eat His flesh and drink His blood will be raised up on the last day (see John 6:54). From a Catholic sacramental and soteriological perspective, we cannot separate the promised Resurrection from the gift of the Eucharist. The Eucharist is the normal means to the Resurrection. Hence, for Father Anastasius to bear the name "Resurrection" is a vivid reminder to all the baptized that the life for which we were made is none other than the life of the Resurrection—the life of intimate communion with the Living God, made possible through the Eucharist.

Do we approach Holy Communion with this awareness, with this conviction? Do we believe that every sacramental Communion is an intensification of the life of intimate communion with the Father and the Son and the Holy Spirit? Reception of Holy Communion is not, or should not be, something we do as a perfunctory gesture. We must do so deliberately and intentionally, with hearts full of joy for so great a Gift!

Chapter 11
Paul Comtois

Martyred February 22, AD 1966
Quebec City, Quebec

IN the play by Robert Bolt about St. Thomas More, *A Man For All Seasons*, St. Thomas said of himself, "This is not the stuff of which martyrs are made."[22] Paul Comtois, the Lieutenant Governor of Quebec from AD 1961 until his death in AD 1966, could easily have used those same words as a description of himself. He was a politician, not a martyr, but as providence would have it, and with an infusion of God's grace, the Honorable Paul Comtois became just that: a martyr, a martyr for the Blessed Sacrament.

Paul Comtois's Catholic faith informed every facet of his personal and public life. Unlike so many politicians today, Comtois did not believe his Catholic faith was an obstacle to being a good politician, something he needed to bracket, but was the impetus for him to seek the common good and to promote the dignity of the human person. Comtois believed he was a good and effective politician because he was a believing, practicing Catholic. Especially key to understanding Comtois's personal and public life was his devotion to the Blessed

[22] *A Man For All Seasons*. Written by Robert Bolt and directed by Fred Zinnemann. Columbia Pictures, 1966.

Sacrament. His devotion to the Blessed Sacrament prevented his faith from being merely an intellectual endeavor but brought him face-to-face with the God-Man, Jesus Christ. His faith was deeply personal because it was in the Person of Jesus, whom he encountered intimately in the Blessed Sacrament.

It is not customary for private residences to receive permission from a bishop to reserve the Blessed Sacrament. And yet Paul Comtois requested this permission from the cardinal archbishop of Quebec for Bois-de-Coulonge, the 105-year-old official residence for the Lieutenant Governor. Initially, the cardinal was disinclined to grant permission, but he eventually gave permission with this caveat: that the Lieutenant Governor himself ensure the protection of the Blessed Sacrament, a responsibility that Comtois graciously accepted and embraced. Comtois made frequent visits to his Eucharistic Lord, especially before retiring for the night.

Sometime around midnight on February 22, a fire broke out in the mansion, aggressively devouring the century-old home. Paul was first to discover the fire, and he immediately began evacuating his family and guests. For some reason, Paul's daughter wanted to return to the burning house, but her father strictly forbade her. Even as he forbade her, he himself ran into the conflagration. It was the last time his family saw him alive.

Paul Comtois reentered the mansion for one reason: to save the Blessed Sacrament in his private chapel. There are two versions as to what happened next. According to one report, Paul Comtois retrieved the pyx containing the consecrated Hosts and began descending the stairs to exit the building when the stairs collapsed and the Lieutenant Governor fell to his death, with his body covering and protecting the pyx, which was discovered by the firefighters.

A second version described Comtois's attempt to open the tabernacle to retrieve the pyx as unsuccessful. He rescued a relic, but upon descending the stairs, they collapsed, and Comtois fell into the fire below and died.

Whether he actually retrieved the pyx or failed to do so, Paul Comtois's love for the Blessed Sacrament caused him to do what he did. He died out of love for his Eucharistic Lord.

Reflection

Firefighters are trained to enter a burning building when others instinctively flee the fire. Paul Comtois had no such training as a firefighter, and yet he overcame the natural urge for self-preservation and ran into the burning residence to preserve the Blessed Sacrament. What can account for his actions, when every fiber of our being tells us to run from the fire, not run into it? Love is the answer. His love for Jesus Christ, truly present in the Blessed Sacrament, alone can explain what he did and why he did it.

The fire consuming the residence can be seen symbolically, in a sense, as the fire that burned within Paul Comtois's heart. Paul Comtois was indeed on fire—on fire with the love of Jesus Christ. He opened his heart to His divine love present in the Holy Eucharist. This fire of divine love perfected his human love. Divine love begets love. Love transforms love. It transformed Paul Comtois into a martyr for the Eucharist.

Chapter 12

FATHER GEORGE WEINMANN

Died February 22, AD 1967

SISTER LILIAN MARIE MCLAUGHLIN, SSND

Died February 20, AD 1967
Rochester, New York

CARDINAL John O'Connor, the archbishop of New York, gave a talk to the seminarians at his *alma mater*, St. Charles Borromeo Seminary in Philadelphia, in the early 1990's. His opening remark was: "The first law of humanity is self-preservation; the first law of the priesthood is preservation of the Eucharist." Approximately twenty-five years prior to this remark, a priest of the neighboring diocese of Rochester and a religious sister bore the ultimate witness to the supreme importance of the Holy Eucharist by offering their lives in an attempt to save the Eucharist from a raging fire.

Shortly after noon on Monday, February 20, AD 1967, an arsonist set fire to St. Philip Neri Church in Rochester, New York.

Noticing the fire, the pastor, Father George Weinmann, rushed into the building to rescue the Blessed Sacrament. Though fire and smoke were everywhere, Father Weinmann made his way to the tabernacle. He had a key to the tabernacle on his key ring and was able to remove the Blessed Sacrament.

About this same time, Sister Lilian Marie, a member of the School Sisters of Notre Dame and a second-grade teacher at the school, ran into the church in search of any children who might be inside. Finding none, she then saw Father Weinmann near the tabernacle and went to help him in his efforts to save the Blessed Sacrament. With each passing moment, the fire grew more intense, and the smoke thickened. If they did not know where the exit was from memory, they would not be capable of discerning it through the smoke.

As Father Weinmann carried the ciborium with the Blessed Sacrament, assisted by Sister Lilian Marie, the two of them were overwhelmed by the smoke and collapsed about six feet from the exit. The ciborium containing the Blessed Sacrament was found by the firefighters next to Father Weinmann, prostrate in the church and barely alive.

Sister Lilian Marie died at the scene of smoke inhalation, while Father Weinmann died two days later on February 22, AD 1967.

The Mass of Christian Burial was presided over by the Bishop of Rochester, Bishop Fulton J. Sheen; he honored both Sister Lilian Marie and Father Weinmann with the designation "martyrs of the Blessed Sacrament." The Bishop said of Sister Lilian Marie: "Martyrs belong to our own times and in most unexpected moments. Sister Lilian Marie gave her life in helping Father Weinmann save the Blessed Sacrament from fire. Greater love than this no woman hath." Bishop Sheen honored Father Weinmann as "a martyred priest in behalf of his Blessed Lord."[23]

---

23 A Different Fire: St Philip Neri (website), "Faith, Fire, & Heroism," accessed February 19, 2024, https://nerifire.wordpress.com/the-st-philip-neri-fires-rescuing-the-blessed-sacrament/.

Reflection

Cardinal O'Connor said the first law of the priesthood is preservation of the Holy Eucharist. In actuality, while priests have a particular responsibility to preserve the Blessed Sacrament from harm or desecration, it is by no means the exclusive purview of priests. All baptized Catholics share in this responsibility, as exemplified by Sister Lilian Marie coming to the aid of Father Weinmann in saving the Blessed Sacrament. But in order for the baptized to so act, it presumes they know and believe the Blessed Sacrament is what It is. We have entered into a period of Eucharistic crisis; far too many Catholics, for whatever reason, deny or simply do not understand the sacred reality of this great Sacrament. Just as Father Weinmann and Sister Lilian Marie had to contend with the smoke that obscured their vision, so a "smoke" has entered into the life of the Church, obscuring the vision of many of who the Eucharist is. A partial remedy for the Eucharistic crisis is Eucharistic education, Eucharistic preaching, and Eucharistic devotional practices; these will help dissipate the smoke, which will lead, pray God, to a renewal in Eucharistic awareness and Eucharistic amazement.

Become a "Eucharistic missionary" in your parish by witnessing through your words and your deeds to the incredible mystery of the Holy Eucharist; ask the Lord for opportunities or "divine appointments" to witness to the blessed reality of the Holy Eucharist.

Part Three

Those Who Risked Their Lives for the Most Blessed Sacrament

Chapter 1
SAINT HYACINTH, OP

Incident November or December, AD 1240
Kiev, Poland

ATOP Bernini's colonnade encircling St. Peter's Square at the Vatican is a ten-feet, four-inch-tall statue of St. Hyacinth, known as "the Apostle to Poland" and "the Apostle of the North" In his right hand, as is typical in religious art of St. Hyacinth, he is holding a small monstrance. Directly across from the statue of St. Hyacinth is the statue of his spiritual father, St. Dominic. How fitting that Bernini's colonnade positions these two spiritual giants across from each other because it was in Rome, in AD 1220, that St. Hyacinth met St. Dominic and personally witnessed the holy founder raise to life the nephew of Cardinal Orsini, who had died in an accident. St. Hyacinth was so moved by the miracle that, on the spot, he and St. Ceslaus, possibly Hyacinth's brother or perhaps his cousin, asked to be received into the Order of Preachers. St. Dominic gave them the holy habit and then proceeded to instruct the two for several months in the spirituality and the vision of the nascent Order of Preachers.

Filled with zeal for the salvation of souls, something St. Dominic imparted to St. Hyacinth and all within his order, Hyacinth returned to his native Poland, founding various Dominican houses.

Between November 28 and December 6, AD 1240, the Mongols attacked the city of Kiev, where St. Hyacinth was on assignment. Prior to this attack, the Mongols had invaded and captured many cities and lands. Their reputation certainly preceded them.

On the fateful day the Mongols attacked Kiev, St. Hyacinth was celebrating the Holy Sacrifice of the Mass. At the conclusion of Mass, he was informed of the dire situation. He knew what could happen if he and the brothers fell into the hands of the Mongols. Immediately and instinctively, however, St. Hyacinth's only consideration was retrieving the Blessed Sacrament from the chapel to prevent Its profanation. Rushing to the chapel's tabernacle, without removing his vestments, St. Hyacinth clutched the ciborium, with its most precious Contents, and pressed it against his heart. As he fled the monastery chapel, a beautiful voice caused Hyacinth to stop: "Hyacinth, my son, will you leave me behind to be trampled underfoot by the [Mongols]? Take me with you." The voice came from a large alabaster statue of Our Lady. Hyacinth replied: "O Holy Virgin, how can I? Your image is too heavy." Our Lady said to him: "Take me anyway. My Son will lighten the burden."

With the ciborium in one hand, Hyacinth miraculously picked up the large statue with his other arm and, without effort, carried the Blessed Sacrament and Our Lady's statue to safety. In so doing, St. Hyacinth was willing to die a gruesome death at the hands of the Mongols in order to save the Blessed Sacrament and the image of Our Lady.

Perhaps as an expression of Our Lady's favor of St. Hyacinth, and in recognition of his great love of Our Lady, St. Hyacinth entered eternal life on the solemnity of the Assumption, August 15, AD 1257, the liturgical commemoration of Our Lady's entrance into heaven, body and soul.

St Hyacinth was canonized by Pope Clement VIII in AD 1594.

Reflection

In the section on the Eucharist in the *Catechism of the Catholic Church*, St. Irenaeus, a Doctor of the Church, is quoted: "Our way of thinking is attuned to the Eucharist and the Eucharist in turn confirms our way of thinking."[24] How could St. Hyacinth immediately and instinctively consider the protection of the Blessed Sacrament once he realized the danger was imminent? No one had to suggest this to him, and he did not have to reason his way to the decision to act. Immediately and instinctively, he knew what had to be done, and without any hesitation, he acted.

St. Hyacinth acted so promptly because he thought eucharistically; his heart and mind were attuned to the Eucharist, and so everything in his priestly life, every decision he made, went through that sacred prism of Jesus really and truly present in the Blessed Sacrament. St. Hyacinth could do nothing other than act to save the Blessed Sacrament.

This way of thinking became connatural with his existence. His personal devotion to the Blessed Sacrament, the countless hours upon hours he spent in private prayer and adoration, formed him and shaped him. His heart and mind were transformed. As St. Paul counsels in Romans 12:2, "be transformed by the renewal of your mind," St. Hyacinth was so changed that his mind and heart were all consumed with the Divine Presence in the Sacrament of the Altar.

Do we think "eucharistically"? Are we so transformed that the priority to preserve the Blessed Sacrament from any and all harm is a part of our consciousness and subconsciousness? The only way to be thoroughly imbued with "eucharistic thinking" is to spend time in His Presence.

---

24 *Catechism of the Catholic Church*, no. 1327.

Chapter 2

Saint Paschal Baylon, OFM

Incident c. AD 1585
France

TRADITIONALLY, the solemnity of Pentecost commemorates the birthday of the Church. In AD 1540, Pentecost fell on May 16, and it also commemorated another birthday: the birthday of a future saint, Paschal Baylon. Such a propitious birth seemed to foreshadow great things for this child of the Spirit.

Though materially poor, he and his family were spiritually rich. From Paschal's youngest years, he manifested, well beyond his age, a profound devotion to Jesus in the Blessed Sacrament. This devotion would characterize his life henceforth and almost cost him his life.

As a youngster, he helped his father with the cattle and eventually did the same with others' herds in order to contribute to the family's finances. He enjoyed the work as it lent itself to a quiet, reflective life, enabling him to contemplate the mysteries of the Faith.

Paschal entered the Franciscan Order as a brother at the age of twenty-four and rapidly grew in grace and virtue. Though his superiors wished he would pursue the holy priesthood, Paschal did not believe that was his vocation within the Order of St. Francis. Instead, Paschal worked in the monastery's garden, served as porter, cook, and was appointed as the one who would go into the city to beg for food and other alms needed by the monastery. He was known for his humility and his cheerfulness, as well as the sage advice he offered to those who sought his counsel.

Paschal's pleasant disposition no doubt originated through his intense life of prayer, especially prayer before the Blessed Sacrament. Most of his free time was spent before the tabernacle, often prostrate in a cruciform or with arms outstretched; often he was found rapt in ecstasy. Many a night he spent in prayer before the Blessed Sacrament. His life truly revolved around Jesus in the Blessed Sacrament. To illustrate his devotion to the Blessed Sacrament, once while outside the monastery, the church bells rang, indicating the moment of the consecration in the Mass. He knelt down in adoration of the Real Presence. Two angels, bearing a beautiful monstrance, appeared before the kneeling Paschal, permitting him to see the One he adored.

Though Brother Paschal had not received formal theological training, he could expound the mysteries of the Faith with great clarity and insightfulness. This was due to the gift of the Holy Spirit called understanding, and Pascal excelled in it. He penetrated the mysteries of the Faith because the Holy Spirit gave him insight, and he freely shared his insights with others. One day, the year is not known, Brother Paschal was traveling through France when he came upon a Calvinist preacher. In the course of their conversation, the Calvinist attacked the doctrine of the Real Presence. Brother Paschal, enlightened by the Holy Spirit and emboldened by that same Spirit through fortitude, engaged the Calvinist preacher with Scriptural arguments clearly establishing the truth of the doctrine of the Eucharist.

The Calvinist preacher, as well as the attending Huguenot crowd, was enraged at the logic and persuasiveness of his arguments. It is reminiscent of what happened to St. Stephen in the Acts of the Apostles. Brought before the Sanhedrin, St. Stephen quoted extensively from the Old Testament, proving Jesus is who Christians say He is, and proving He fulfilled everything in the Mosaic law. The crowd refused to listen and Stephen called them "stiff-necked" (Acts 7:51). The very same can be said about Brother Pascal and the Huguenot crowd. Just as Stephen was martyred for his faith in the Person of Jesus Christ, so the crowd turned on Paschal and wanted to kill him for defending the Blessed Sacrament so eruditely. He barely escaped with his life, but if God had willed his martyrdom, of rendering the definitive witness in his blood, Paschal would have accepted God's will with joy. Pascal's will was only to do the will of God.

Brother Paschal died on May 17, AD 1592, after falling ill. He was canonized by Pope Alexander VIII in AD 1690.

Reflection

St. Paschal demonstrates the profound connection between the Holy Spirit and devotion to the Blessed Sacrament. Jesus breathed forth the Holy Spirit in His dying breath on the Cross (see Jn 19:30). The Spirit is given to us to reveal Jesus Christ. Just as "no one can say 'Jesus is Lord' except by the Holy Spirit" (1 Cor 12:3), so no one can recognize His presence except by the Holy Spirit; it is a corollary. Jesus taught the very same at the conclusion of the Bread of Life discourse when He said: "It is the Spirit that gives life" (Jn 6:63). Without the Spirit, human nature cannot penetrate the mysteries of Faith.

The Holy Spirit is the Great Revealer. He overshadowed Our Lady, and the Word was made flesh. The Holy Spirit is invoked in every Mass that Jesus may be made really and truly present under the appearance of bread and wine. When a person is baptized, the Holy Spirit causes the divine life to be made present in the soul of the baptized.

Do you want to have the faith of a martyr? Do you want to see beyond the appearance of bread and see Jesus Christ Himself? Then cultivate a devotion to the Holy Spirit.

Chapter 3

Firefighter Leroy McAtee and Captain H. H. Buddy Edwards

Incident March 19, AD 1954
Mobile, Alabama

THE police were making their customary patrol in downtown Mobile on Friday, March 19; the patrol area included the cathedral of the Immaculate Conception, the center of Catholic life in the Archdiocese of Mobile, Alabama. At 2:55 a.m., the police noticed smoke bellowing out of the century-old majestic building and immediately called it in as a fire in progress.

It was a three-alarm fire, and crews from all over the city converged on the inferno, hoping to extinguish it quickly and save the beautiful church dedicated to Our Lady. Apparently, a homeless man gained entrance into the cathedral's basement and, under the influence of alcohol, lit a fire there in an attempt to warm himself.

A total of twenty-seven water lines were used in the three-hour effort to subdue the flames. The acting Fire Chief, Dan Sirmon, stated it was the most difficult fire to contain in Mobile's history.

Msgr. Timothy J. Pathe, the cathedral rector, appeared on the scene, and his first thought was to retrieve the Blessed Sacrament from the conflagration. Firefighters forbade him to enter the cathedral. "I have to save the Blessed Sacrament," pleaded the rector. Two firefighters responded to his plea: Firefighter Leroy McAtee and Captain Buddy Edwards. Providentially, the two had been altar servers and were familiar with the layout of the cathedral; that would be important because of the black smoke obstructing their vision. Additionally, having served Mass there for so many years, they knew where the key to the tabernacle was kept—important since they would need to retrieve the Blessed Sacrament. Msgr. Pathe instructed the two firefighters that the tabernacle contained two ciboria and a luna, which contained the consecrated large Host for exposition and benediction.

The two firefighters, amid flames and intense heat and black smoke everywhere, began working their way toward the high altar. McAtee first retrieved the tabernacle key. The firefighters recalled the floor beneath them was growing hotter and hotter. Time was of the essence. Then he and Edwards opened the tabernacle and recovered the Blessed Sacrament: two ciboria and the luna. No sooner had the two firefighters accomplished this sacred task and began heading outside when the floor upon which they stood to retrieve the Blessed Sacrament fell through and opened up a large cavity into the consuming fire below. Had they delayed even a couple of seconds, they would have fallen victim to the fire.

The two successfully navigated the harrowing path to safety, whereupon they entrusted to the apprehensive monsignor the precious Body of the Lord in the Blessed Sacrament. Monsignor Pathe expressed his profound appreciation for their personal devotion to the Blessed Sacrament and for their willingness to put their own lives in jeopardy to save Jesus. Receiving the ciboria and the luna from the hands of the firefighters, Monsignor and an accompanying priest hurried off to the chapel inside the chancery, only one block from the fire, to secure the Blessed Sacrament.

Archbishop Thomas J. Toolen expressed his personal gratitude for the heroism of the firefighter Leroy McAtee and Captain Edwards.

Reflection

The fire occurred in the early hours of March 19, which is also the liturgical celebration of St. Joseph. St. Joseph was chosen by Divine Providence to watch over and protect Jesus, the Bread of Life. In this sense, St. Joseph was foreshadowed by Joseph the Patriarch, the son of Jacob and Rachel, in the Old Testament. Joseph was betrayed by his brothers and taken as a prisoner into Egypt. Through a series of providential events, Joseph gained the favor of the pharaoh and was given charge of all the stored wheat in Egypt, in preparation for a future famine. He was the protector of the wheat. When the famine struck, it affected the whole land, including his brothers. When the people complained to the pharaoh that they needed wheat to make bread for their sustenance, his response was "Go to Joseph" (Gn 41:55).

"Go to Joseph," the great protector of the wheat, the one entrusted with the earthly bread for life, and he will feed you with sustenance for this life. St. Joseph, however, is the real protector of the Bread of Life; he is the one entrusted with heavenly Bread for divine life.

Though the two firefighters on their sacred mission to save the Bread of Life did not mention being guided by St. Joseph, he must have been there, guiding each step they took, preventing harm to them and especially harm to the One he protected while he lived. Now, from heaven, St. Joseph still protects the Bread of Life.

Should anyone desire to grow in greater devotion to the Blessed Sacrament, then "go to Joseph."

Chapter 4
VENERABLE FRANCIS-XAVIER NGUYỄN VĂN THUẬN[25]

Incidents April 15, AD 1975–November 21, AD 1988
Hanoi, Vietnam

HE had been a priest for twenty-two years and a bishop for seven when Francis-Xavier Nguyễn Văn Thuận was arrested on the solemnity of the Assumption in AD 1975 and imprisoned by the Communist government of Vietnam. The Communists banished him to what was euphemistically called a "re-education camp." There he was imprisoned for the next thirteen years, nine of which he spent in solitary confinement, because he was a Catholic bishop who preached the Gospel of Jesus Christ and the dignity of human life.

In an interview after his release in AD 1988, the bishop was asked if he had been able to celebrate Mass while in prison. The bishop replied "it is a question I have been asked many, many times. And when I say 'Yes', I can foretell the next question, 'How did you get the bread and wine?'"

---

[25] A reference to Venerable Francis-Xavier Nguyễn Văn Thuận's interview can be found here: "The Eucharist: My Only Strength." https://www.ctsbooks.org/the-eucharist-my-only-strength/.

"I was taken to prison empty-handed. Later on, I was allowed to request the strict necessities like clothing, toothpaste, etc. I wrote home saying 'Send me some wine as medication for stomach pains'. On the outside, the faithful understood what I meant.

"They sent me a little bottle of Mass wine, with a label reading 'medication for stomach pains', as well as some hosts broken into small pieces.

"I will never be able to express the joy that was mine: each day, with three drops of wine, a drop of water in the palm of my hand, I celebrated my Mass.

"At 9:30 every evening when the lights went out, I bent over my wooden board and celebrated Mass, by heart of course, and distributed Communion to my neighbors under their mosquito nets. We made tiny bags from cigarette paper to protect the Blessed Sacrament.

"At night, the prisoners took turns and spent time in adoration. The Blessed Sacrament helped tremendously. Even Buddhists and other non-Christians were converted. The strength of the love of Jesus is irresistible. The darkness of the prison became a paschal light.

"Many friends have asked me, 'What is your secret strength that enabled you to survive prison?' The strength that empowered me was the Eucharist."

In order for Văn Thuận to celebrate the Mass as he did during his imprisonment, he did so at the very real risk of being killed if discovered. But for the bishop, life without the Eucharist was already death. Simply put: no Eucharist, no life. The Eucharist enabled him to persevere in faith, hope, and charity. The Eucharist reinvigorated his life.

Francis-Xavier Nguyễn Văn Thuận was released from prison on November 21, AD 1988, and placed under house arrest. In AD 1991, he was expelled from Vietnam and never permitted to return. His new home became Rome. Pope St. John Paul II elevated

Văn Thuận to the cardinalate in AD 2001. He died in Rome on September 16, AD 2002.

After the mandatory five-year waiting period following a person's death, his cause for canonization was opened in Rome. Pope Francis declared him Venerable on May 4, AD 2017.

Reflection

Is the Eucharist the center of my life? Do I excuse myself from coming to the Eucharist as though it is not that important? What sacrifice can I make that is too great for the Sacrifice Jesus made for me and which comes to me in the Eucharist?

Francis-Xavier Nguyễn Văn Thuận was willing to be a martyr of the Eucharist, and the reason he was so inclined was because he lived every day of his life for the Eucharist. He lived because of the Eucharist. He lived in the Eucharist. The Eucharist was the center of his life, as it must be for our lives. For Francis-Xavier Nguyễn Văn Thuận, the supreme truth of existence is: Jesus Christ is really and truly present in the Eucharist. He is there; He is really there.

Part Four

Other Deaths Connected with the Most Blessed Sacrament

Chapter 1
Blessed Imelda Lambertini

Died May 12, AD 1333
Val di Pietra, Italy

SHE died at the young age of eleven, and yet her short life manifested a vibrant faith, an intense hope, and an ardent charity, especially an incredible awareness and love of Jesus in the Most Blessed Sacrament. Those who knew Magdalen Lambertini, her baptismal name, could not help but be impressed by her virtuous life and moved by her prayerfulness, devotion, and witness to the Real Presence.

Born in AD 1322 in a town close to Bologna, Italy, where St. Dominic is buried and enshrined, Magdalen grew up in a devout Catholic family. Her parents instilled in their daughter a tremendous love for the Catholic faith. The young girl, well beyond her chronological age, seemed to grasp difficult truths of the Faith and penetrate into their meaning—an awareness that many adults did not possess. Her understanding proceeded from her love. The more she loved, the more that was revealed to her; and the more that was revealed to her, the greater her love grew. Love and understanding form a symbiotic relationship, as seen in Magdalen.

Magdalen had two great "hungers" in her life: a hunger for a life of intimate prayer and a hunger to receive Jesus in the Most

Blessed Sacrament. To feed her hunger for prayer and intimacy with God, Magdalen made a "chapel" in a corner of her home where she retired and spent hours in contemplation. As to her second hunger, to receive Holy Communion, at this time in Church history, the customary age for First Holy Communion was fourteen, and little Magdalen was only five years old; she begged and pleaded with her parents for permission. Poor Magdalen was told she had to wait nine more years! For a five-year-old, that must have seemed like an eternity. Magdalen, however, did not stop making the same request over and over; her pastor was asked about the possibility, and he too dismissed the request as if the child did not really understand what she was asking. Ironically, she did know, and that awareness, caused by love, fueled her desire and incessant requests.

Magdalen's love and desire for Jesus in the Blessed Sacrament caused her to wonder and to ask others, "How is it possible to receive Jesus into one's heart and not to die?"[26] Far from having an immature understanding of the great Gift present in the Blessed Sacrament, as her pastor suggested, Magdalen grasped the mystery of Faith and longed for this Gift with all her heart.

Shortly after Magdalen turned nine years old, she approached her parents with yet another request: that she be permitted to live with nuns and adopt their way of life and prayer insofar as she could at that age. Her parents discussed the idea and agreed to entrust their precious Magdalen to the Dominican nuns in Val di Pietra. Magdalen was ecstatic to join the nuns and quickly advanced in grace, virtue, and holiness. The nuns were impressed with their little sister.

Though Magdalen could not make canonical vows at such a young age, she nevertheless gave herself to the Dominican life as best she could. The nuns gave her a little Dominican habit to wear,

---

26 Catholic Kingdom (website). "Blessed Imelda Lambertini." Accessed February 19, 2024. https://www.catholickingdom.com/AAA_load_in_pages/Monastery/Lives%20of%20the%20Saints/Female/Blessed_Imelda.html.

and Magdalen chose for herself a religious name; henceforth, she was to be called Imelda.

As happy as Imelda was to be with the nuns, she still longed for Holy Communion. When the nuns approached the Communion rail to receive Jesus, Body, Blood, soul, and divinity, Imelda wept. How she longed to receive Jesus in Holy Communion!

On May 12, AD 1333, the Vigil of the Ascension of Jesus into heaven, when Imelda was eleven years old, she was again overwhelmed with the need to receive Jesus in the Blessed Sacrament. She pleaded that she be allowed this stupendous Gift; and again, her pleadings were rebuffed. After the Holy Mass concluded, Imelda remained in the chapel immersed in prayer, pouring out her desire and her love for the Eucharistic Lord.

As Imelda continued in prayer, a heavenly fragrance permeated the chapel and from the chapel to the nuns' enclosure. Curious as to the source of this beautiful fragrance, the Sisters discovered it emanated from their little Imelda. As they gazed on her rapt in prayer, a light shone above Imelda, and in the light, a sacred Host was clearly visible. The astonished nuns quickly called for the priest to come and witness the miracle. The priest was inspired to bring a paten and for some time adored Jesus in the Host suspended above Imelda. Gradually, the Host descended and rested on the priest's paten. It was clear what the priest must do: he must administer to the eleven-year-old her first Holy Communion with the miraculous Host. As the priest said to Imelda, "*Corpus Christi*," her Eucharistic Lord entered her heart and soul and found a worthy recipient, despite her youthfulness. Imelda was filled with even greater love for Jesus than she had ever known before. Truly, in this graced moment, her tiny heart and His Sacred Heart melded into one. And then, unaware of the depth of this mystical communion, the nuns discovered Imelda, with a beatific smile on her face and a countenance that conveyed her intense love, had been transported by love and through love to the One who is Love-in-the-flesh! Imelda was taken from this life, in which her Jesus hid behind the appearance of bread, to the life of perfect joy, where she saw her Jesus face-to-face.

Imelda, who has been called "the Flower of the Eucharist," was beatified by Pope Leo XII on December 20, AD 1826. Pope St. Pius X named her patron saint for First Communicants in AD 1910.

Reflection

Imagine we would only receive Jesus in the Blessed Sacrament one time in life. Imelda spent eleven years preparing for her one and only reception of Communion; and she now spends the rest of eternity in thanksgiving for this Gift of the Savior! How do we prepare to receive Jesus in Holy Communion? Do we take time asking for the grace of a worthy and fruitful Holy Communion? Do we take time after Holy Communion to thank the Lord Jesus Christ for coming into our hearts and souls?

We would do well to turn to Blessed Imelda every time we are to receive the Blessed Sacrament, asking for her intercession that our hearts and souls are properly prepared.

Chapter 2
SAINT MARGARET CLITHEROW

Martyred March 25, AD 1586
York, England

THE information for the life of St. Margaret Clitherow comes from her confessor and friend, Father John Mush; he wrote a biography of her about three months after her death. Her date of birth is not known with certainty, but it is generally believed she was born circa AD 1553.

St. Margaret was the daughter of Thomas Middleton, the sheriff of York. She was one of four children, all of whom were raised in the Church of England. Her parents were probably Catholics who left the Faith not for theological reasons but for reasons of convenience and aspirations for social advancement.

One of the few dates known with certainty about St. Margaret is that of her wedding. She was married to John Clitherow on July 8, AD 1571. John was a butcher who later, because he adopted the Queen's religion, was eligible to become an elected official; Catholics by law were ineligible. He was subsequently elected to various positions and became relatively prominent in York.

At the time of their wedding, John and Margaret were both Protestant, though John had a brother who became Catholic and even a priest, Father William Clitherow. In AD 1574, three years after her marriage to John, Margaret became Catholic. Fr. Mush gave the reason: she "found no substance, truth nor Christian comfort in the ministers of the new church, nor in their doctrine itself, and hearing also many priests and lay people to suffer for the defense of the ancient Catholic Faith."[27]

Despite the difference in religion, John admired his wife for her devotion, her conviction, and her Christian example. Of his wife, John said, "Alas, will they kill my wife? Let them take all I have and save her, for she is the best wife in all England and the best Catholic."

As a Catholic, Margaret thirsted for prayer and discovered that her prayer life was key to entering more intimately into communion with Jesus. She spent an hour and a half every day in prayer and meditation and was devoted to reading the Sacred Scriptures. Among other books she admired, her favorite was *The Imitation of Christ* by Thomas a Kempis. Margaret had a great love for Our Lady too, and she prayed the Little Office of Our Lady daily.

Margaret and John had three children, two boys and one girl. One of the boys was named after John's brother, William, the priest; their other son was named Henry. Their one daughter was named Anne. All three, with John Clitherow's permission, were raised as Catholics by Margaret, and in fact, the two sons became priests, and the daughter became a nun.

St. Margaret requested that after her death, her shoes be sent to her daughter, Anne, with the message that she was to follow in her footsteps and remain faithful to Catholicism.

While Margaret was married to John and after she became a Catholic, the law imposed a fine on every subject who absented himself from attending the worship service created by the Queen and her ministers. To John Clitherow's credit, he uncomplainingly paid the fine so that Margaret could attend Mass. Soon though, the

---

27 "St. Margaret Clitherow." http://www.savior.org/saints/clitherow.htm#:~:text=Mush%2C%20Margaret%20became%20a%20Catholic,John%20Clitherow%2C%20remained%20a%20Protestant.

penalty for the crime of attending Mass became imprisonment, and Margaret was convicted for this crime more than once. In fact, one of her sons, William, was born while in prison. Records indicate that she spent two years in prison for going to Mass, as well as other shorter periods.

Margaret used her numerous times in prison to go deeper in prayer, a kind of retreat for her. Though the cells were damp and dark and vermin-infested, and many prisoners died due to the harsh environment, Margaret delighted in spending time with her Lord in prayer. While in prison she taught herself to read and learned various devotions that were unknown to her as a Protestant. All that she learned through her reading and all that she learned through her prayerful intimacy with the Lord, she brought back home and shared with her children.

Her one sorrow was that John was not open at all to the Catholic faith. That which brought her the greatest joy was something she could not share with the man she loved so dearly. But Margaret knew her love for her husband could not keep her from her love for Jesus and His Church. Fortunately, she was not in a position that she had to choose one over the other, but the pain she experienced at not being able to share this with John was an on-going sacrifice she made.

Margaret, without involving her husband in the plans, converted the house into a sanctuary for the celebration of the Mass and a sanctuary for priests, who, if caught, would die a most gruesome death by evisceration.

Within Margaret's house were hiding places for the wine used for Mass, the unconsecrated hosts, sacred vestments, and sacred vessels. The house also contained what is called a "priest hole," that is, a secret hiding place for priests. There was also a secret passage that connected the Clitherow house to the neighbor's house, which allowed priests to flee undetected.

Given John Clitherow's growing prestige, including the position he acquired one year after their marriage of being a reporter to London of any "rebels and other evil-disposed persons suspected of Papistry," and given Margaret's increasing outspokenness about Catholicism, authorities often searched the Clitherow residence in York in hopes of finding incriminating articles connected with the celebration of the Mass.

Margaret also rented a room some distance away from her house that could hide priests too. Margaret loved priests, for from them, we have the gift of the Most Holy Sacrament. All of this, the secret hiding places for the Mass vestments, the secret hiding place for priests, the room she rented also to hide priests, was unknown to her husband. Whenever Mass was celebrated, it was done so that not even John Clitherow knew about it. All of this was to protect her husband.

In AD 1585, Parliament enacted a law called "27 Elizabeth." No longer was assisting at Mass a crime punishable by a fine or imprisonment. It was declared an act of treason punishable by death. St. Margaret Clitherow was one of the first arrested and charged under this new law.

On March 12, AD 1586, while John was away and Margaret was busy doing housework, two sheriffs arrived at the Clitherow house to search it yet again. The initial search, like so many before it, yielded nothing. Before leaving, the sheriffs discovered several children in a room being taught school lessons by a man. The man was thought to be a priest. He was not, but confusion ensued with the teacher escaping. The children were detained by the authorities for questioning. Not all of them were Margaret's children, since she opened her home to other Catholic families who wished to receive a Catholic education.

One boy, eleven years old, new to the Clitherow house, was utterly terrorized by the sheriffs, and before long, the boy revealed the hiding place of priests, as well as the hiding place for all the items used in the celebration of the Mass. Margaret was immediately arrested, as were the children, but they were soon released.

While in prison, Margaret, awaiting almost certain death, was happy, always seen with a smile. Her jailers were dumbfounded and could not comprehend her attitude; no one before her acted as she did. She encouraged the others in prison to cling to their faith. In many ways, St. Margaret's conduct in prison was similar to another Catholic martyr imprisoned for being Catholic: St. Maximillian Kolbe.

Margaret knew in her spirit that this imprisonment and likely execution was an answer to her prayers. Margaret actually prayed for the grace of martyrdom. Before her imprisonment, under cover of night, Margaret would make a secret pilgrimage to pray at the gibbet, not far from her home, that was used to kill priests, several of whom she knew personally and for whom she had provided a hiding place. Martyrdom was, in St. Margaret's mind, the natural response and expression of self-surrender to Him who gave all for us and was received in the Eucharist.

While in prison, Margaret was brought before judges several times; to no avail they tried to convince her to embrace the Queen's religion. On the third day of imprisonment, her husband, John, was permitted to visit briefly with her. He also tried to convince her to forsake Catholicism, but Margaret knew to deny her faith would be to deny her very identity. For Margaret, being Catholic was existential; it was not incidental. Each reception of the Eucharist intensified the bond of communion with the Lord Jesus; He defined her very existence, and since He is truly present in the Eucharist, that sacrament was integral to her identity. She could no more deny her faith than she could voluntarily stop breathing.

On Monday, March 14, in the evening, Margaret was once again brought before several judges. This time she was formally charged, and the indictment read: she was charged with harboring priests and attending Mass. She was asked to plead. This is an interesting point of English law.

Margaret's response caught her judges off guard. She did not assert her innocence nor did she admit guilt. She did not plead at all. Rather, she declared: "Having made no offense, I need no trial."

Not to plead at all to an indictment carried with it an automatic death penalty, and the penalty was to be "pressed to death." This barbaric form of execution required a person to lay on the ground with a sharp rock, about the size of a fist, under his back while a large board, much like a door, would cover the person and one by one, stones and weights would be added until the person was pressed to death.

Margaret's choice not to plead was motivated by this fact: if she did not plead, then there could not be a trial, and if there were no trial, then her husband, her children, her servants, and her friends could not be called to testify against their mother and their friend. And if they did not testify, then they could not blame themselves for her death. Margaret could not bear the thought that her husband and children would be manipulated by the courts and inserted into the drama of her death sentence. She knew she would be killed regardless. Margaret's choice not to plead was a final act of charity for those she loved.

The judge warned Margaret that if she refused to plead, her death would be far worse than if she was found guilty by a jury. She would not plead. Margaret was sent back to prison for the night in the hope that she would reconsider.

The next morning found her back before the judge, and again, she refused to plead. He begged her, and others did as well. Being pressed to death, having almost all the bones in one's body broken slowly by the pressure of added weights, was a most gruesome and painful death.

After her refusal, the judge condemned her to death by pressing. Margaret declared to the court: "I will accept willingly everything that God wills." The sentence was to be carried out in ten days' time. Upon hearing of the sentence of death for his wife, John wept bitterly. Father Mush, Margaret's confessor and biographer, described John in this way: "He wept so violently that blood gushed out of his nose." John informed the judge that Margaret was pregnant. That made no difference to the judge.

March 25 arrived. Affectionately called "Lady Day" in England, this was the feast of the Annunciation, the day God the Son took on human flesh and became a baby in the precious womb of Our Lady. March 25 marks the beginning of our salvation; for Margaret, it would be the day of her birth into eternal life.

At eight o'clock in the morning, Margaret was led, like a lamb to the slaughter, to her place of execution. Those who saw her remarked about her joyful, smiling countenance. Margaret was escorted by two guards, four executioners, and four women friends. She walked barefooted with her burial shroud, which she made the previous night, draped over her arm. Upon arriving at the place of execution, the guards instructed Margaret to completely disrobe. She knelt and pleaded she be spared this humiliation, but they refused.

Margaret, still kneeling, began to pray aloud for the pope, her country, and her Queen; her prayer was that she would return to the Catholic faith. The sheriff, for one last time, gave Margaret the opportunity to confess to her crimes. Margaret answered the sheriff: "No, no, Mr. Sheriff, I die for the love of my Lord Jesus."

In the thirty-third year of her life, on the feast of the Incarnation, Margaret was stripped of her clothes and laid upon the ground in a cruciform. Her arms were tied to stakes. The sharp rock was placed under her back, and then the large wooden board covered her. The weights were added, one by one, until it totaled over eight hundred pounds. Margaret opened not her mouth in complaint. The only words heard from her lips were: "Jesus, Jesus, Jesus, have mercy on me."

After fifteen minutes of unbearable torture, bones snapping, suffocation, internal bleeding, Margaret died. No doubt at that moment she heard the words of Jesus: "Arise, my love, my fair one, and come" (Sg 2:10).

On October 25, AD 1970, Pope Paul VI canonized her as "the Pearl of York." She was canonized with thirty-nine others, known collectively as "the Forty English and Welsh Martyrs."

Reflection

From St. Margaret's example, we discover that the Mass, the inestimable Gift of the Eucharist, is something for which we should be willing to die before renouncing or trivializing it as not important. Do we value the Mass to this degree? Do we appreciate the Mass as the means by which God draws us to the Cross of Jesus and draws the Cross of Jesus to us?

The Holy Sacrifice of the Mass is the greatest assistance we have to personal growth in holiness. If we enter into each and every Mass with our whole being, if we enter into each part of the Mass with greater consciousness and active participation, then the potential for transformation is virtually unlimited! We cannot become saints today without devotion to the Eucharist and the Mass.

Chapter 3
SAINT ANNE LINE

Martyred February 27, AD 1601
Tyburn, England

IMAGINE living in world in which simply being a Catholic priest was a capital offense; imagine, too, that in this world, any person who hosted a priest in one's home or hid a priest from the authorities was guilty of a capital offense. That was the world in which Anne Line lived. But what is so amazing in the case of Anne Line is that it was a world into which she knowingly entered. Anne chose to become Catholic at a time when practicing the Catholic faith in England was illegal and punishable even by death.

At her birth, she was given the name Alice by her Protestant parents. Her father was a leading Puritan, and her grandfather helped King Henry VIII in "reforming" the Church in England. When Alice announced to her family, sometime in the 1580's, that she, her brother William, and her husband Roger were entering into the Catholic Church, they were summarily disinherited from the family. At her reception into the Church, Alice took the name Anne, in honor of the mother of the Mother of God. From that point on, she was known as Anne.

Her disinheritance soon became a real issue since her husband, Roger, and her brother were arrested for attending the Holy Mass;

her brother was eventually released, but Roger was exiled from England. For a short time, Anne received some monetary support from her exiled husband, but this ended when Roger died. Anne was on her own all because she became Catholic.

As a devout Catholic, Anne's life revolved around attending the Holy Sacrifice of the Mass, even if it could only be celebrated clandestinely and sporadically. She discerned a call, with the help of the Jesuit Father John Gerard, to help the priests who were risking their lives in order to celebrate the Holy Mass and to bring the faithful the Holy Eucharist. She conducted "safe houses" for the celebration of Mass and for priests to hide to elude discovery and capture, a fate that meant certain death.

The authorities had Father Gerard under surveillance, and his familiar association with Anne Line caused her too to become a person of interest. On the Feast of the Presentation of the Lord in the Temple, also known as Candlemas since candles are blessed in the Mass, February 2, AD 1601, a large number of the Catholic faithful arrived at her home to participate in the secret Mass. The sheer number of people arriving at this house was enough to arouse suspicion, and the authorities were alerted that an illegal Mass might be underway.

The authorities responded quickly, but Anne was prepared. The priest, Father Francis Page, was able to remove his vestments and blend in among the laity. With the chaos that ensued in searching the house, most everyone was able to escape, including Father Page. (Father Page, however, would be discovered about a year later and was martyred for being a priest on April 20, AD 1602; he was beatified on December 15, AD 1929, by Pope Pius XI.) The authorities did discover the altar and arrested Anne Line for suspicion that she had hidden, or was hiding, a priest. She was imprisoned in Newgate Prison until her trial on February 26, AD 1601. Without evidence that she had, in fact, hidden a priest, Anne was found guilty and sentenced to death by hanging, a sentence to be carried out the next day. After her sentence was announced, Anne chose to discharge her conscience. She admitted to helping priests, and her only regret was that she could not have helped more than she did.

Before her execution was carried out, Anne repeated her statement at her trial: "I am sentenced to die for harboring a Catholic priest, and so far I am from repenting for having so done, that I wish, with all my soul, that where I have entertained one, I could have entertained a thousand!"[28] What holy boldness!

On February 27, AD 1601, Anne was hanged in the presence of two priests who were themselves to be hanged, drawn, and quartered: Father Mark Barkworth, OSB and Father Roger Filcock, SJ, who was also Anne's confessor.

After Anne died, and before she was removed from the scaffold, Father Filcock kissed the hem of her dress and declared: "Oh blessed Mrs. Line, who has now happily received thy reward, thou art gone before us, but we shall quickly follow thee to bliss, if it please the Almighty."[29]

She was canonized by Pope St. Paul VI on October 25, 1970, as one of the Forty Martyrs of England and Wales.

Father Mark Barkworth was beatified by Pope Pius XI on December 15, 1929, and Father Roger Filcock was beatified November 22, AD 1987, by Pope St. John Paul II.

Reflection

St. Anne Line's witness to the supreme importance of the Most Holy Eucharist, as revealed in her protection of priests, is particularly instructive in a time when, according to a recent Pew Research

---

[28] Diocese of Westminster [UK] Youth Ministry (website), "Saint Anne Line: Defiant in the Face of Death," accessed February 19, 2024, https://youth.rcdow.org.uk/discover/anne-line/.

[29] Stephanie Mann, "Candlemas and Four English Martyrs," Eternal Word Television Network, February 2, 2017, https://ewtn.co.uk/article-candlemas-and-four-english-martyrs/.

survey, faith in the Real Presence among self-identifying Catholics is at a historic low. If the Eucharist is not what the Church says it is, the real and substantial Body and Blood of Jesus, then St. Anne Line died a fool's death. She died for wishful thinking. But if the Eucharist is, as Jesus Himself declared in the Gospel, His actual Body and Blood, then how can anything in life surpass its importance? Her death magnifies the reality of the Holy Eucharist and Its supreme importance in her life, in the life of the Church, and indeed in the life of the world.

For St. Anne Line, to protect the priests, who are the very means by which the Eucharist is made present, was her way of ensuring the perpetuation of the Eucharist since it is impossible to have that Sacrament apart from priests. Do we regularly pray for our priests? Do we beseech God to keep priests pure and holy? Do we pray for an increase in vocations to the sacred priesthood?

Chapter 4
SAINT NICHOLAS OWEN, SJ

Martyred March 2, AD 1606
London, England

ST. Nicholas Owen, though physically a small man in stature, was a giant of a man spiritually speaking. His life story is the stuff of which action-adventure films are made.

Nicholas was one of four sons born to devout Catholic parents. Two of his brothers became priests, a traitorous act at that time in English history; the other brother became a printer and engaged in printing Catholic literature, deemed subversive and hence a felonious act. Nicholas followed in the footsteps of his father by becoming a master carpenter, a skill that he ingeniously used for the protection of priests and thus the preservation of the Most Holy Eucharist. *Butler's Lives of the Saints* introduced its article on St. Nicholas Owen with this extraordinary claim: "Perhaps no single person contributed more to the preservation of the Catholic religion in England during the penal times than a humble artisan called Nicholas Owen, who in the reign of James I saved the lives of many priests by his extraordinary skill in devising hiding places for them."[30]

[30] Herbert Thurston and Donald Attwater, ed., *Butler's Lives of the Saints*, Vol. 1 (Westminster, MD: Christian Classics), 579.

Nicholas committed his life and his God-given talents to ensure the faithful in England would have the Most Holy Eucharist and the other sacraments by protecting the priests from the "priest-hunters." He accomplished this sacred task by the construction of "priest holes," hiding places in the homes of Catholics for priests and the sacred vestments and vessels required for the celebration of the Holy Mass. He built these hiding places into the floors, ceilings, walls, and chimneys. Nicholas's design and construction were so masterful that experts today believe that some priest holes have yet to be discovered. No two priest holes were the same. Some could accommodate a single priest, while others could accommodate as many as ten. Many of the priest holes had tunnels attached to them so the priest could safely vacate the premises into a remote area where the entrance to the tunnel was cleverly camouflaged by Nicholas Owen. Some of the priest holes constructed by Nicholas were meant to be discovered in an attempt to throw off the priest-hunters from the real priest hole often hidden behind the phony one.

The priest-hunters, in searching a specific home, brought their own carpenters in an attempt to discover and expose the work of Nicholas Owen. However, they were seldom successful.

Before Nicholas began a new priest hole, he first attended Holy Mass and received the Blessed Sacrament; it was his way of consecrating the project to the Lord Jesus, the Great High Priest, beseeching His wisdom and guidance as he endeavored to protect His priests. Nicholas worked only at night so no one, other than the owner of the house, would know the location of the priest hole.

In AD 1581, Nicholas Owen was arrested for the first time, not in connection with constructing priest holes but because he came to the public defense of the Jesuit Father Edmund Campion. Nicholas entered into the service of Father Campion and through this association became friends with him. He knew the law that forbade priests from ministering was unjust and hence not a valid law. Father Campion was tortured and martyred on December 1, AD 1581.

After Father Campion's martyrdom, Nicholas Owen entered into the service of the Jesuit superior in charge of missions in England, Father Henry Garnet. In AD 1588, Father Garnet wrote a letter in which he expressed his sincerest desire that "his carpenter" would be permitted entrance into the Society of Jesus. Though not specifically named, it is believed Father Garnet was referring to Nicholas Owen. At some point after his letter, Nicholas Owen was admitted to the Society as a lay brother.

Brother Nicholas was again arrested and tortured on April 23, AD 1594, though the officials did not know at that time that Brother Nicholas was "*the* carpenter" responsible for constructing priest holes all over England. Eventually, after disclosing nothing to the officials, Brother Nicholas was released. When Brother Nicholas was arrested, so was Jesuit Father John Gerard. Father Gerard stood trial and was found guilty and consequently imprisoned; throughout his imprisonment, he was regularly tortured in a futile effort to extract information from him about the priests in England. On October 4, AD 1597, Father Gerard escaped the Tower of London; it is believed Brother Nicholas orchestrated his escape. Father Gerard lived until AD 1637, when he died at seventy-three years of age.

As a result of the foiled "Gunpowder Plot" of AD 1605, priest-hunters diligently sought out priests and their collaborators who were believed to have played some part in planning the Plot. In December, AD 1605, Brother Nicholas, Brother Ralph Ashley, Father Garnet, and Father Edward Oldcorne were forced into hiding as priest-hunters searched for them. After several days of searching the house in which they were hiding, Brother Nicholas and Brother Ralph emerged from hiding in the hopes their discovery would dupe the priest-hunters into believing no one else was present. It was not successful, and eventually all four were apprehended and arrested.

Once it was realized who Brother Nicholas was, his interrogation was particularly intense and gruesome. For several successive days, Brother Nicholas was racked for hours at a time. As he refused to divulge any of the locations of the priest holes he constructed, their frustration and fury intensified, as did his torture. Brother Nicholas suffered from a hernia, and during his torture it eventually ruptured, and his agony was indescribable. His captors incorporated his ruptured hernia into the ongoing torture; what they did to Nicholas was truly demonic. Yet, throughout this horrific ordeal, Brother Nicholas never uttered a word. He died from these tortures in the early hours of March 2, AD 1606.

Nicholas Owen was canonized by Pope St. Paul VI in October, AD 1970, as one of the Forty Martyrs of England and Wales. Father Edward Oldcorne and Brother Ralph Ashley were beatified as martyrs by Pope Pius XI on December 15, AD 1929.

Reflection

Someone may judge the adage "it only takes one person to make a difference" as more of a cliché than a description of fact, and yet history shows that one person can indeed make an enormous difference, as is the case with St. Nicholas Owen. Untold scores of priests would not have survived were it not for Brother Nicholas. He truly made a profound difference.

Perhaps another example will prove the adage can reflect historical fact. Sometime around AD 400, a hermit living in the East believed God spoke to him and commanded he go to Rome for a mission—a mission that was not described. The hermit's name was Telemachus. Walking the entire way on foot, the trek took weeks and weeks. On entering the great capital of the world, Telemachus heard wild, almost delirious shouts. As he came closer to the source of all the commotion, he was face-to-face with the infamous coliseum. The shouts were discernable: "Kill him! Kill him!" Horrified, Telemachus entered the coliseum and witnessed a gladiatorial contest. Two men, armed with swords, were engaged in a mortal combat.

His undisclosed mission now became clear: he had to stop the senseless killing of human life. Telemachus made his way down to the dirt floor of the coliseum. The shouting and the screaming continued. How could he be heard over this cacophony of noise? When he opened his mouth, he felt a force welling up in him. He shouted in a voice the Lord clearly amplified: "Stop in the name of Christ! Stop the killing!" He was heard. The fight temporarily halted. The audience listened to the old man dressed in a long robe. "Stop, I say, in the name of Jesus Christ!" The protestation of Telemachus was met with laughter and jeers from the gladiators. All eyes were upon this new confrontation. One of the gladiators approached Telemachus, drew his sword, and dispatched the hermit effortlessly. The horrified audience fell silent as they witnessed the barbarity of the murder, and one by one the audience exited the coliseum in stupefied silence. It would be the last gladiatorial fight in the coliseum. Telemachus, in his death, made a difference, a difference that changed an empire.

Just like St. Nicholas Owen, one person can make a difference with enormous consequences. The power of change, the power to make a real difference, resides not in one's personal attributes, but in the docility to let the power of Jesus Christ work in His disciples. Without Christ, we can do nothing of consequence; with Him, we can do the unimaginable. Every person reading this book can be like St. Telemachus and St. Nicholas Owen and make a real, substantive difference. And the biggest difference will come from our fidelity to our Catholic faith and to the Real Presence of Jesus Christ in the Eucharist. If each person lives his or her faith without compromise, we will make a difference.

Conclusion

A Meditation on the Institution of the Most Holy Eucharist

BY way of conclusion, I offer a meditation on the Institution of the Most Holy Eucharist through the eyes of Jesus. It is my hope that in seeing through His eyes, our hearts will be imbued with a renewed Eucharistic Amazement and see this Great Sacrament as the greatest act of love possible.

So, let us begin this meditation.

Jesus is in the Upper Room; the meal is about to begin. His head is bowed; His eyes are closed as He prays intensely to His Father. The Apostles notice that look of intensity; it is a look they have witnessed many times over the last three years. But something seems different about Him. Peter motions to John to ask Jesus if He is alright, when, at that moment, Jesus raises His head, He opens His eyes, and sees the table prepared for the Passover with the Festival Light burning brightly.

The Festival Light is lit by the mother of the household. How many times He and His foster father, Joseph, and His blessed Mother celebrated this sacred ceremony together. He can still see Mary's face as the Festival Light shone upon her.

He loves His Mother beyond human expression. She gave Him His human nature, which in a few hours will be subject to such torture and cruelty that He will barely be recognizable as being human. Through her "fiat" at the Annunciation, salvation began as the Word was made flesh and dwelt among us.

Just the thought of Mary brings a tear to His eyes. She loves Him as no other person could, for her Heart is Immaculate. There is no sin in her, no selfishness; she loved as human beings were meant to love.

He knows she will be with Him tomorrow, not only watching and praying, but she will also renew her "fiat" to His self-offering to the Father; insofar as she is able as His Mother, she will be united with her Son. As she has lived her life, so now, at this supreme moment in human history, she unites her heart to the Father's heart and offers her dear, dear Son to Him.

Jesus's Heart aches for her as He knows what she will suffer tomorrow. A sword of sorrow will pierce her Immaculate and Sorrowful Heart. Jesus must provide for her as He will be taken from her. He says to Himself, "I will give her to John, My beloved Apostle. He will take care of her as his very own mother." John, though, stands in for all Christians, for Mary is our Mother too; how can she not be, if her Son is born within us by grace? When someone is baptized, she is there, giving her fiat again that the Word may be made flesh in the baptized soul.

Next, Jesus lowers His head, and now His eyes rest upon the lamb and the unleavened bread.

He recalls what John the Baptist said of Him: "Behold the Lamb of God, who takes away the sin of the world" (Jn 1:29). He is that Lamb. And just as the Passover lamb had to be slain, its blood sprinkled and its flesh eaten, so Jesus, the True Lamb of God, must be slain. His precious Blood must be applied, not to the lintels of doors, but to our lips; His flesh, too, must be eaten. To this end, Jesus promised during the previous Passover that He would give us His flesh to eat under the appearance of bread. "I am the living bread which came down from heaven. . . . the bread which I shall give for the life of the world is my flesh . . . My flesh is food indeed, and my blood is drink indeed" (Jn 6:51, 55).

Jesus is the Lamb. The Passover lamb in front of Him is a symbol, a symbol pointing to Jesus Himself. Jesus will take our sins upon Himself. He will offer Himself, body, blood, soul, and divinity, to the Father on our behalf. As the true Lamb, He takes all our sins to the Cross. He bears them in His body. He confesses these sins to the Father upon the Cross in groanings we cannot understand. And on Easter Sunday morning, He receives for us the gift of absolution from the Father as life returns to His dead body. Isn't that what happens in the sacrament of confession? We receive the new life of the Resurrection.

Jesus then hears whispering and turns to see it is Peter. What a generous heart beats in this man, but a heart that is still very much in the grip of fear: fear of suffering, fear of self-donation, fear of the unknown. "O, how I have prayed for you, Peter! I know, even if you don't, what you are capable of with My grace in your heart. You will do great things for Me, Peter, even if at this moment you cannot."

Sitting across from Peter, Jesus sees Judas. Jesus's eye tears again, not because of the physical suffering that awaits Him, but because Jesus thirsts for love, and you, Judas, have closed your heart to His Heart. "O, Judas, how could you have been with Me for so long now and still not let My love penetrate the hardness of your heart? But Judas, even though you will betray Me for thirty pieces of silver, it is not unforgiveable. No one, in this life, is ever beyond the power of My grace and mercy.

"Judas, how can you think there is no hope, no forgiveness? How can My sacrifice on the Cross not be enough for you? What more could I have done that I did not do? All that I am, I give: in the Eucharist, on the Cross, to all that will accept My love. That is all I ask: To respond to My love with love, and to those that do I will refuse nothing, for they will be immersed in My Sacred and

Merciful Heart, their heart beating within Mine and My Heart beating in theirs."

Jesus's Heart is torn as He sees His love spurned by Judas.

Jesus closes His eyes for a moment, realizing that His Hour has arrived, the Hour for which He was born, the Hour the Father set for Him to reconcile all humanity to His divine love. The Father does this by giving us the Son and the Son by giving us Himself, all of Himself. Jesus opens His eyes again, ready to fulfill the Father's will; He picks up the bread and says, "Take, eat; this is my body" (Mt 26:26).

Appendix 1

LITANY OF THE BLESSED SACRAMENT[31]

Lord, have mercy.
Christ, have mercy.
Lord, have mercy.
Christ, hear us.

Christ, graciously hear us.
God the Father of Heaven, have mercy on us.
God the Son, Redeemer of the world, have mercy on us.
God, the Holy Spirit, have mercy on us.
Holy Trinity, One God, have mercy on us.

O Living Bread, Who from Heaven descended, have mercy on us.
Hidden God and Savior, have mercy on us.
Grain of the elect, have mercy on us.
Vine sprouting forth virgins, have mercy on us.
Wholesome Bread and delicacy of kings, have mercy on us.
Perpetual sacrifice, have mercy on us.
Clean oblation, have mercy on us.
Lamb without spot, have mercy on us.

---

[31] Litany of the Most Blessed Sacrament. https://www.preces-latinae.org/thesaurus/Euch/LitDeSS.html.

Most pure feast, have mercy on us.
Food of Angels, have mercy on us.
Hidden manna, have mercy on us.
Memorial of God's wonders, have mercy on us.
Supersubstantial Bread, have mercy on us.
Word made flesh, dwelling in us, have mercy on us.
Holy Victim, have mercy on us.

O Cup of blessing, have mercy on us.
O Mystery of faith, have mercy on us.
O Most high and venerable Sacrament, have mercy on us.
O Most holy of all sacrifices, have mercy on us.
O True propitiatory Sacrifice for the living and the dead, have mercy on us.
O Heavenly antidote, by which we are preserved from sin, have mercy on us.
O stupendous miracle above all others, have mercy on us.
O most holy Commemoration of the passion of Christ, have mercy on us.
O Gift transcending all abundance, have mercy on us.
O extraordinary memorial of Divine love, have mercy on us.
O affluence of Divine largess, have mercy on us.
O most holy and august mystery, have mercy on us.

Medicine of immortality, have mercy on us.
Awesome and life-giving Sacrament, have mercy on us.
Unbloody Sacrifice, have mercy on us.
Food and guest, have mercy on us.
Sweetest banquet at which the Angels serve, have mercy on us.
Bond of love, have mercy on us.
Offering and oblation, have mercy on us.
Spiritual sweetness tasted in its own fountain, have mercy on us.
Refreshment of holy souls, have mercy on us.
Viaticum of those dying in the Lord, have mercy on us.

Pledge of future glory, have mercy on us.

Be merciful, spare us, O Lord.
Be merciful, graciously hear us, O Lord.

From the unworthy reception of Thy Body and Blood, deliver us, O Lord.
From passions of the flesh, deliver us, O Lord.
From the concupiscence of the eyes, deliver us, O Lord.
From pride, deliver us, O Lord.
From every occasion of sin, deliver us, O Lord.
Through that desire with which Thou desiredst to eat the Passover with Thy disciples, deliver us, O Lord.
Through that profound humility with which Thou didst wash Thy disciples' feet, deliver us, O Lord.
Through that most ardent love with which Thou instituted this Divine Sacrament, deliver us, O Lord.
Through the most precious Blood, which Thou hast left for us upon the altar, deliver us, O Lord.
Through those Five Wounds of Thy most holy Body, which was given up for us, deliver us, O Lord.

Sinners we are, we beseech Thee, hear us.

That Thou wouldst graciously preserve and augment the faith, reverence, and devotion in us towards this admirable Sacrament, we beseech Thee, hear us.
That Thou wouldst graciously lead us through the true confession of our sins to a frequent reception of the Eucharist, we beseech Thee, hear us.
That Thou wouldst graciously free us from every heresy, falsehood, and blindness of the heart, we beseech Thee, hear us.
That Thou wouldst graciously impart to us the Heavenly and precious fruits of this most Most Holy Sacrament, we beseech Thee, hear us.

That Thou wouldst graciously protect and strengthen us in our hour of death with this Heavenly Viaticum, we beseech Thee, hear us.

O Son of God, we beseech Thee, hear us.

Lamb of God, Who taketh away the sins of the world, spare us, O Lord.
Lamb of God, Who taketh away the sins of the world, graciously hear us, O Lord.
Lamb of God, Who taketh away the sins of the world, have mercy on us, O Lord.

Christ, hear us.
Christ, graciously hear us.

Lord, have mercy.
Christ, have mercy.
Lord, have mercy.

Our Father . . .

Hail Mary . . .

V. Thou didst furnish them with Bread from Heaven.

R. Having in it every delight.

Let us pray: O God, Who under a marvelous Sacrament has left us a memorial of Thy Passion; grant us; we beseech Thee; so to venerate the sacred mysteries of Thy Body and Blood, that we may ever perceive within us the fruit of Thy Redemption. Thou, Who livest and reignest forever and ever. Amen.

Appendix 2

Scriptural Passages for Meditation before the Blessed Sacrament

OPENING Prayer: O Holy Spirit, You are the Great Revealer of Jesus Christ. Reveal Him now to me as I come before His Real Presence in the Most Blessed Sacrament. I ardently desire to render Him perfect praise and worship, but in my poverty, I realize I cannot. Come, Holy Spirit, and accompany me in this journey into His Sacred and Eucharistic Heart. Speak to my heart through Your inspired words in Sacred Scripture. Reveal Jesus and the depth of His love to me. Help me to love Him and adore Him with greater devotion than I have ever had. Amen.

[After each verse, pause a few moments, reflecting on the words of Scripture as they "paint" a portrait of Jesus, a portrait to be revealed to those who adore His Eucharistic Face.]

"Cast all your anxieties on him, for he cares about you" (1 Pt 5:7).

"Holy, holy, holy is the LORD of hosts; the whole earth is full of his glory" (Is 6:3).

"Then flew one of the seraphim to me, having in his hand a burning coal which he had taken with tongs from the altar. And he touched my mouth, and said: 'Behold, this has touched your lips; your guilt is taken away, and your sin forgiven'" (Is 6:6–7).

"'And his name shall be called Emmanuel' (which means, God with us)" (Mt 1:23).

"For to you is born this day in the city of David a Savior, who is Christ the Lord" (Lk 2:11).

"You will find a babe wrapped in swaddling cloths and lying in a manger" (Lk 2:12).

"And going into the house, [the Magi] saw the child with Mary his mother, and they fell down and worshiped him" (Mt 2:11).

"And the Word became flesh and dwelt among us" (Jn 1:14).

"Mine eyes have seen thy salvation" (Lk 2:30).

"Thou art my beloved Son; with thee I am well pleased" (Lk 3:22).

"The next day [John the Baptist] saw Jesus coming toward him, and said, 'Behold, the Lamb of God'" (Jn 1:29).

"I am the bread of life; he who comes to me shall not hunger" (Jn 6:35).

"I am the living bread which came down from heaven; if any one eats of this bread, he will live for ever; and the bread which I shall give for the life of the world is my flesh" (Jn 6:51).

"He who eats my flesh and drinks my blood abides in me, and I in him" (Jn 6:56).

"This is my body which is given for you. Do this in remembrance of me" (Lk 22:19).

"When he was at table with [the two disciples on the road to Emmaus], he took the bread and blessed, and broke it, and gave it to them. And their eyes were opened and they recognized him; and he vanished out of their sight. They said to each other, 'Did not our hearts burn within us while he talked to us'" (Lk 24:30–32).

"My Lord and my God!" (Jn 20:28).

"Lord, to whom shall we go? You have the words of eternal life; and we have believed, and have come to know, that you are the Holy One of God" (Jn 6:68–69).

"It is witnessed of him, 'Thou art a priest for ever, after the order of Melchizedek'" (Heb 7:17).

"Come to me, all who labor and are heavy laden, and I will give you rest" (Mt 11:28).

"On his robe . . . he has a name inscribed, King of kings and Lord of lords" (Rv 19:16).

"I am the Alpha and the Omega, the first and the last, the beginning and the end" (Rv 22:13).

"Lo, I am with you always, to the close of the age" (Mt 28:20).

[Take a few moments and speak to Jesus in your own words. Tell Him of your love and your desire to live each day of your life in intimate communion with Him. Finally, ask Our Lady, Mother of the Eucharist, to help you grow in this love and in Eucharistic Amazement.]

References

Pope Saint Sixtus II

The Catholic Encyclopedia, s.v. "Valerian." Accessed February 20, 2024. www.newadvent.org/cathen/15256b.htm.

The Catholic Encyclopedia, s.v. "Pope St. Sixtus II." Accessed February 20, 2024. www.newadvent.org/cathen/14031c.htm.

Saint Edmund Gennings and Companions

Barry, Patrick. "The Penal Laws." Eternal Word Television Network. https://www.ewtn.com/catholicism/library/penal-laws-1704.

Bilyeau, Nancy. "Little Ease: Torture and the Tudors." http://englishhistoryauthors.blogspot.com/.

The Catholic Encyclopedia, s.v. "Edmund and John Gennings." Accessed February 20, 2024. http://en.wikisource.org/wiki / Catholic_Encyclopedia_(1913)/Edmund_and_John_Gennings.

———, s.v. "Ven. Swithin Wells." Accessed February 20, 2024. http://www.newadvent.org/cathen/15580b.htm.

Hickey, Julia A. "Richard Topcliffe-Torturer." *The History Jar*, February 28, 2014. https://thehistoryjar.com/2014/02/28/anish-topcliffe-torturer/.

Kelly, Christine J. “Saint Edmund Gennings.” In *Oxford Dictionary of National Biography.* https://www.oxforddnb.com/display/10.1093/ref:odnb/9780198614128.001.0001/odnb-9780198614128-e-10516. DOI: https://doi.org/10.1093/ref:odnb/10516.

Lyons, Mathew. “Richard Topcliffe: The Queen’s Torturer.” *Matthew Lyons: Writer and Historian* (blog), June 25, 2012. http://mathewlyons.wordpress.com/2012/06/25/richard-topcliffe-the-queens-torturer/.

Tertullian, *Apologia*. Accessed February 22, 2024. https://www.newadvent.org/fathers/0301.htm.

Wikipedia, s.v. “Richard Topcliffe.” Accessed February 22, 2024. http://en.wikipedia.org/wiki/Richard_Topcliffe.

Saint John Roberts, OSB

The Catholic Encyclopedia, s.v. “St. John Roberts.” Accessed February 20, 2024. http://www.newadvent.org/cathen/13098c.htm.

Mann, Stephanie A. “Execution at Tyburn Tree.” *Supremacy and Survival: The English Reformation* (blog), December 10, 2011. http://supremacyandsurvival.blogspot.com/2011/12/anish-10-1610-executions-at-tyburn.html.

Wikipedia, s.v. “John Roberts.” Accessed February 22, 2024. http://en.wikipedia.org/wiki/John_Roberts_(martyr).

Blessed William Southerne

Catholic Daily Readings (website). “Blessed William Southerne–Saint of the Day–April 30.” Accessed February 12, 2024. https://catholicreadings.org/blessed-william-southerne-saint-of-the-day-april-30/.

The Catholic Encyclopedia, s.v. “Venerable William Southerne.” Accessed February 20, 2024. http://www.newadvent.org/cathen/14162a.htm.

Encyclopedia.com, s.v. "Blessed William Southerne." Accessed February 22, 2024. www.encyclopedia.com/religion/encyclopedias-almanacs-transcripts-and-maps/southerne-william-bl.

Blessed Thomas (John Baptist) Bullaker, OFM

Mann, Stephanie A. "Blessed Thomas Bullaker, OFM." *Supremacy and Survival: The English Reformation* (blog), October 12, 2011. http://supremacyandsurvival.blogspot.com/2011/10/blessed-thomas-bullaker-ofm.html.

Ridgeway, Johnathan. "The Blessed Martyrs of Sussex." *Catholic Saints* (blog), October 3, 2014. http://latinsaints.wordpress.com/2014/10/03/the-blessed-martyrs-of-sussex/.

Schofield, Nicholas. "The English Franciscan Martyrs." *Roman Miscellany* (blog), June 24, 2007. http://romanmiscellany.blogspot.com/2007/06/english-franciscan-martyrs.html?m=0.

Wood, Steven. "The Franciscan Martyrs of England." Accessed February 16, 2024. https://stevenwood.com/reflections/franciscan/0504-34.htm.

Servant of God Leo Heinrichs, OFM

"Priest Shot Dead at Communion Rail." *New York Times*, February 24, 1908. https://www.nytimes.com/1908/02/24/archives/priest-shot-dead-at-communion-rail-anarchist-glories-in-crime.html.

Jenkins, William Rev. "Martyr of the Holy Eucharist." Reprinted from *The Roman Catholic*, with permission in 2007. https://stpiusvchapel.org/pdf-site/articles/fr_leo.pdf.

Saint Oscar Romero

Cavanaugh, William T. "Dying for the Eucharist or Being Killed by It?: Romero's Challenge to First-World Christians." *Theology*

Today 58, no. 2 (2001): 177–189. http://www.jesusradicals.com/uploads/2/6/3/8/26388433/dying-for-the-eucharist.pdf.

Super Martyrio. "Archbishop Romero on All Saints' Day." Super Martyrio, October 31, 2010. https://polycarpi.blogspot.com/2010/10/.

The Archbishop Romero Trust. http://www.romerotrust.org.uk.

Vatican Council II. Dogmatic Constitution on the Church *Lumen Gentium*. November 21, 1964.

Catholics in Iraq

Assyrian Information Management (website). "Islamic Terrorists Kill Assyrians in Baghdad Church." October 31, 2010. http://www.atour.com/news/assyria/20101031a.html.

Chulov, Martin. "Baghdad Church Siege Survivors Speak of Taunts, Killings and Explosions." *Guardian*, November 1, 2010. http://www.theguardian.com/world/2010/nov/01/baghdad-church-siege-survivors-speak.

Shadid, Anthony. "Church Attack Seen as Strike at Iraq's Core." *New York Times*, November 1, 2010. http://www.nytimes.com/2010/11/02/world/middleeast/02iraq.html?pagewanted=all.

Fournier, Keith. "Catholics Killed at Mass in Iraq: Extremist Muslims Invade Church, Murder Priests." Catholic Online (website), November 2, 2010. http://www.catholic.org/news/international/middle_east/story.php?id=38976.

Leland, John. "In Grief and Defiance, Baghdad's Christians Return to Scene of Attack." *New York Times*, November 7, 2010. http://www.nytimes.com/2010/11/08/world/middleeast/08baghdad.html?_r=1&.

Wikipedia, s.v. "2010 Baghdad Church Massacre." Accessed February 16, 2024. http://en.wikipedia.org/wiki/2010_Baghdad_church_attack.

Servant of God Jacques Hamel

Caldwell, Zelda. "A martyr's death: Fr. Jacques Hamel is remembered." *Aleteia* (blog),July 26, 2021. https://aleteia.org/2021/07/26/a-martyrs-death-fr-jacques-hamel-is-remembered/.

Zinos, Nicholas. "Father Jacques Hamel, Europe's First 21st-Century Martyr." *America: The Jesuit Review*, July 26, 2018. www.americamagazine.org/faith/2018/07/26/father-jacques-hamel-europes-first-21st-century-martyr.

Saint Tarcisius

The Catholic Encyclopedia, s.v. "St. Tarsicius." Accessed February 20, 2024. www.newadvent.org/cathen/14461a.htm.

The Editors. "St. Tarcisius: A Model of Faithfulness to the Lord." August 20, 2010. https://www.ncregister.com/news/st-tarcisius-a-model-of-faithfulness-to-the-lord.

St. Justin Martyr. *First Apology*. Accessed February 20, 2024. https://www.newadvent.org/fathers/0126.htm.

Stevens, Clifford. "St. Tarcisius." Taken from *The One Year Book of Saints*. Huntington, IN: Our Sunday Visitor, 2005. https://www.ewtn.com/catholicism/library/st-tarcisius-5890

Saint Hermenegild

A Man For All Seasons. Written by Robert Bolt and directed by Fred Zinnemann. Columbia Pictures, 1966.

Britannica, s.v. "Leovigild." Accessed February 16, 2024. http://www.britannica.com/EBchecked/topic/336722/Leovigild.

Butler, Alban. *The Lives of the Fathers, Martyrs, and Other Principal Saints*. Vol. 4. Dublin: James Duffy, 1866. Accessed February 16, 2024. http://www.bartleby.com/210/4/131.html.

Catholic Saints (website). "Saint Hermenegild." Accessed February 16, 2024. http://www.catholic-saints.info/roman-catholic-saints-h-l/saint-hermenegild.htm.

New World Encyclopedia, s.v. "Arius." Accessed February 16, 2024. http://www.newworldencyclopedia.org/entry/Arius#cite_note-0.

The Gorkum Martyrs

Blessed George *The Catholic Encyclopedia*, s.v. "The Martyrs of Gorkum." Accessed February 20, 2024. https://www.newadvent.org/cathen/06651c.htm#:~:text=These%20were%3A%20Nicholas%20Pieck%2C%20guardian,Franciseus%20de%20Roye%2C%20of%20Brussels.

———, s.v. "St. Nicholas Pieck." Accessed February 20, 2024. http://www.newadvent.org/cathen/11065b.htm.

Catholic Exchange (website). "The 19 Martyrs of Gorkum." Accessed February 19, 2024. www.catholicexchange.com/the-19-martyrs-of-gorkum.

Dominican Friars Foundation (website). "St. John of Gorkum." Accessed February 19, 2024. http://dominicanfriars.org/st-john-of-gorkum/.

Dominican Sisters of St. Cecilia (website). "St. John of Cologne." Accessed February 19, 2024. www.nashvilledominican.org/community/our-dominican-heritage/our-saints-and-blesseds/st-john-of-cologne.

O'Connor, Flannery. *The Habit of Being*. Edited by Sally Fitzgerald. New York: Farrar, Straus and Giroux, 1979.

Wikipedia, s.v. "History of Religion in the Netherlands." Accessed February 19, 2024. http://en.wikipedia.org/wiki/History_of_religion_in_the_Netherlands.

Blessed George Napier (Also Napper)

Catholic Church, *The Liturgy of the Hours*. Vol. 2. page 621.

Collins, Richard. "Martyr, Bl George Nappier." *Linen on the Hedgerow* (blog), November 9, 2010. http://linenonthehedgerow.blogspot.com/2010/11/martyr-bl-george-nappier.html.

Mann, Stephanie A. "Blessed George Napper or Napier." *Supremacy and Survival: The English Reformation* (blog), November 9, 2012. http://supremacyandsurvival.blogspot.com/2012/11/blessed-george-napper-or-napier.html.

Schiffer, Kathy. "Blessed George Napier, Priest and Martyr, Pray for Us." *Patheos* (blog), December 26, 2014. http://www.patheos.com/blogs/kathyschiffer/2014/11/blessed-george-napier-priest-and-martyr-pray-for-us/.

Whitehead, John. "Bl. George Napier 1610–2010." *Once I Was a Clever Boy* (blog), November 8, 2010. http://onceiwasacleverboy.blogspot.com/2010/11/bl-george-napier-1610-2010.html.

Manuel

Soha, Mary. "The Florida Martyrs." Lecture on YouTube, March 14, 2022. https://www.youtube.com/watch?v=4yJqSqs4G0c.

For more information on the cause for canonization of the martyrs of La Florida, visit their website: www.martyrsoflafloridamissions.org.

Blessed Simon Cardon and Companions (Martyrs of Casamari)

Catholic Church, *The Roman Missal.* Totowa: Catholic Book Publishing, 2011.

O'Connor Flannery, *The Habit of Being*. Edited by Sally Fitzgerald. New York: Farrar, Straus and Giroux, 1979.

Order of Cistercians of the Strict Observance (website). "Beatification of the Martyrs of Casamari." April 22, 2021. https://ocso.org/2021/04/22/beatification-of-the-martyrs-of-casamari/.

Peterson, Larry. "The Eucharistic Martyrs of Casamari." *Catholic 365* (blog), January 7, 2021. https://www.catholic365.com/article/12669/the-eucharistic-martyrs-of-casamari.html.

Peterson, Larry. "These Newly Beatified Monks Died Defending the Eucharist." *Aleteia* (blog), April 20, 2021. https://aleteia.org/2021/04/20/these-newly-beatified-monks-died-defending-the-eucharist/.

Saint Cesidio Giacomantonio, OFM

Anonymous. "Dino Sees Great Uncle Cesidio Made Saint." *Catholic Leader* (blog), March 16, 2021. https://catholicleader.com.au/news/ dino-sees-great-uncle-cesidio-made-saint_37135/.

Britannica, s.v. "Boxer Rebellion." Accessed February 19, 2024. http://www.britannica.com/event/Boxer-Rebellion.

Catholic Online. "St. Cesidio Giacomantonio." Accessed February 19, 2024. https://www.catholic.org/saints/saint.php?saint_id=7117.

Martinez, Luis M. *The Sanctifier* (Daughters of St. Paul, 1982).

Saint Pedro Maldonado

Anonymous. "Feast of St. Pedro Maldonado." *Catholic Sun*, February 11, 2019. https://www.catholicsun.org/2019/02/11/feast-of-st-pedro-maldonado/.

Catholic Diocese of El Paso (website). "San Pedro De Jesus Maldonado." Accessed February 19, 2024. https://www.elpasodiocese.org/san-pedro-de-jesus-maldonado.html.

Catholic.net. "St. Peter of Jesus Maldonado." Accessed February 19, 2024. https://catholic.net/op/articles/2151/peter-of-jesus-maldonado.html.

Knights of Columbus (website). "St. Pedro de Jesús Maldonado Lucero." May 20, 2021. https://www.kofc.org/en/news-room/articles/mexicanmartyrs/st-pedro.html.

Najera, Joe and Fabian Marquez. "The Birth of a Saint." Video. Accessed February 19, 2024. https://www.elpasodiocese.org/san-pedro-de-jesus-maldonado.html.

Saint Ignatius Catholic Parish, Mobile, AL (website). "Saint of the Month: St. Pedro Maldonado." Accessed February 19, 2024. https://www.stignatiusmobile.org/saint-of-the-month-st-pedro-maldonado/.

"Li"

Allen, Charlotte. "Little Li: The Child Martyr of the Eucharist in China." Benedict XVI Institute, June 30, 2021. https://benedictinstitute.org/2021/06//little-li-the-child-martyr-of-the-eucharist-in-china/.

My First Holy Communion (website). "Little Li." Accessed February 19, 2024. https://www.myfirstholycommunion.com/portfolio-view/little-li/.

Sheen, Fulton J. *Treasure in Clay*. Doubleday, New York, NY, 1980.

Blessed Janos (Anastasius) Brenner, OCist

Abels, Kelly. "Bl. János Brenner and Our Journeys to Sainthood." *The Cor Chronicle* (blog), November 10, 2021. https://thecorchronicle.com/2021/11/10/bl-janos-brenner-and-our-journeys-to-sainthood/.

Catholic News Agency. "Father Janos Brenner: Hungarian Priest and Martyr." November 11, 2017. https://www.catholicnewsagency.com/news/37177/father-janos-brenner-hungarian-priest-and-martyr.

Fifty-Second International Eucharistic Congress (website), Budapest, 2021. "The Martyr of the Eucharist–János Brenner." April 9, 2018. https://www.iec2020.hu/en/news-press/martyr-eucharist-janos-brenner.

Jacobs, Billy. "Blessed Janos Brenner." *Path to the Sainthood* (blog), September 2, 2020. https://www.thepathtosainthood.com/post/blessed-janos-brenner.

Kosloski, Philip. "Meet Bl. János Brenner, a Martyr of the Eucharist." *Aleteia* (blog), August 29, 2021. https://aleteia.org/2021/08/29/meet-bl-janos-brenner-a-martyr-of-the-eucharist/.

Our Lady of Dallas Cistercian Abbey (website). "Fr. Anastasius John Brenner (1931-1957)." Accessed February 19, 2024. https://abbey.cistercian.org/history/our-saintly-inspiration/fr-anastasius-john-brenner/.

Paul Comtois

Catholicism.org. "A Modern Catholic Hero: Paul Comtois." October 14, 2008. https://catholicism.org/paul-comtois.html.

Cusack, Andrew. "Paul Comtois of Québec: Farmer, Politician, Hero, Saint." Personal blog, March 24, 2009. http://www.andrewcusack.com/2009/paul-comtois/.

de Souza, Raymond J. "Paul Comtois—A Martyr for the Eucharist." *National Post*, March 7, 2016. https://nationalpost.com/opinion/father-raymond-j-de-souza-paul-comtois-a-martyr-for-the-eucharist.

Hoopes, Tom. "They Died for the Eucharist. Would you?" *Aleteia* (blog), August 26, 2019. https://aleteia.org/2019/08/26/they-died-for-the-eucharist-would-you/.

Father George Weinmann and Sister Lilian Marie McLaughlin, SSND

A Different Fire: St Philip Neri Website. "Faith, Fire, & Heroism." Accessed February 19, 2024. https://nerifire.wordpress.com/the-st-philip-neri-fires-rescuing-the-blessed-sacrament/.

Find a Grave (website). "Rev George J Weinmann." Accessed February 19, 2024. http://www.findagrave.com/cgi-bin/fg.cgi?page=gr&GRid=61895503.

———. "Sr Lilian Marie McLaughlin." Accessed February 19, 2024. http://www.findagrave.com/cgi-bin/fg.cgi?page=gr&GSln=mclaughlin&GSfn=lilian&GSbyrel=in&GSdy=1967&GSdyrel=in&GSob=n&GRid=61895609&df=all&.

Saint Hyacinth, OP

Anonymous. "Saint Hyacinth." *Godzdogz* (blog), August 16, 2014. https://www.english.op.org/godzdogz/saint-hyacinth/.

Anonymous. "Saint Hyacinth and Our Lady's Statue." *Dominican Monastery of Our Lady of the Rosary, Summit, NJ* (blog), October 27, 2019. https://summitdominicans.org/blog/2019/10/21/h3l4mrnp4veyrzz7mwhnr97jpkse47.

A Guide to Christian Iconography: Images, Symbols, and Texts (website). "Saint Hyacinth: The Iconography." Accessed February 19, 2024. https://www.christianiconography.info/hyacinth.html.

Peterson, Larry. "St. Hyacinth of Poland; This "Apostle of the North" Saved the Holy Eucharist and the Blessed Virgin from Destruction by Walking Them across a River." *Catholic 365* (blog), September 13, 2019. https://www.catholic365.com/article/10592/st-hyacinth-of-poland-this-apostle-of-the-north-saved-the-holy-eucharist-and-the-blessed-virgin-from-destruction-by-walking-them-across-a-river.htm.

Saint Hyacinth Roman Catholic Church, Detroit, MI (website). "Saint Hyacinth: A Short Account of the Life of Our Patron Saint. Accessed February 19, 2024. https://www.sainthyacinth.com/our-saint.

St Peter's Basilica.Info. "Colonnade Saints." Accessed February 19, 2024. http://stpetersbasilica.info/Exterior/Colonnades/Saints-List-Alphabetical.htm.

The Catholic Encyclopedia, s.v. "St. Hyacinth." Accessed February 20, 2024. https://www.newadvent.org/cathen/07591b.htm.

Saint Paschal Baylon, OFM

Roman Catholic Saints (website). "Saint Paschal of Baylon." Accessed February 19, 2024. https://www.roman-catholic-saints.com/saint-paschal-of-baylon.html.

The Catholic Encyclopedia, s.v. "St. Pascal Baylon." Accessed February 20, 2024. https://www.newadvent.org/cathen/11512a.htm.

Firefighter Leroy McAtee and Capt. H. H. Buddy Edwards

"Cathedral Fire 1 of Toughest." *Mobile Register*. Accessed via Diocese of Mobile Archives.

"Fire Agency Seeks Cause of Big Blaze." *Mobile Register*, March 20, 1954. Accessed via Diocese of Mobile Archives.

"Services at Cathedral Seem Likely Sunday." *Mobile Register*, March 23, 1954. Accessed via Diocese of Mobile Archives.

"Trapped Fireman Saved." *Catholic Week*, March 27, 1954. Accessed via Diocese of Mobile Archives.

Venerable Francis-Xavier Nguyễn Văn Thuận

Mangan, Charles M. "Cardinal Francois-Xavier Nguyen van Thuan: The Lord's True Witness." Catholic Online, 2004. https://www.catholic.org/featured/headline.php?ID=1316.

Martin, Regis. "Cardinal van Thuan—Heroic 'Witness to Hope' Who Spent 13 Years in a Communist Prison." *National Catholic Register* (blog), August 3, 2021. https://www.ncregister.com/blog/cardinal-van-thuan-witness-to-hope.

Landry, Roger. "The Eucharistic Shape of Cardinal Nguyen van Thuan's Holy and Heroic Life." *National Catholic Register* (blog), September 14, 2022. https://www.ncregister.com/blog/eucharistic-shape-of-cardinal-nguyen-van-thuans-life.

Blessed Imelda Lambertini

Catholic Kingdom (website). "Blessed Imelda Lambertini." Accessed February 19, 2024. https://www.catholickingdom.com/AAA_load_in_pages/Monastery/Lives%20of%20the%20Saints/Female/Blessed_Imelda.html.

Dominican Sisters of Saint Cecilia (website). "Bl. Imelda Lambertini." Accessed February 19, 2024. https://www.nashvilledominican.org/community/our-dominican-heritage/our-saints-and-blesseds/bl-imelda-lambertini-2/.

Michael for the Triumph of the Immaculate (website). "Blessed Imelda Lambertini." September 1, 2018. https://www.michaeljournal.org/articles/roman-catholic-church/item/blessed-imelda-lambertini.

Roman Catholic Saints (website). "Blessed Imelda Lambertini." Accessed February 19, 2024. https://www.roman-catholic-saints.com/blessed-imelda-lambertini.html.

Saint Margaret Clitherow

The Catholic Encyclopedia, s.v. "St. Margaret Clitherow." Accessed February 20, 2024. www.newadvent.org/cathen/04059b.htm.

Cruz, Joan Carroll. *Secular Saints*. TAN Books: Rockford, Illinois, 1989.

Saint Anne Line

Diocese of Westminster [UK] Youth Ministry (website). "Saint Anne Line: Defiant in the Face of Death." Accessed February 19, 2024. https://youth.rcdow.org.uk/discover/anne-line/.

Hadley, Cheryl. "St. Anne Line, English Martyr & Protector of Priests and Seminarians." *Catholic Company*, February 25, 2022. https://www.catholiccompany.com/magazine/st-anne-line-english-martyr-protector-of-priests-and-seminarians/.

Mann, Stephanie A. "Candlemas and Four English Martyrs." Eternal Word Television Network, February 2, 2017. https://ewtn.co.uk/article-candlemas-and-four-english-martyrs/.

Saint Nicholas Owen, SJ

de Souza, Raymond J. "St. Nicholas Owen, the Martyred Carpenter Saint of the English Persecution." *National Catholic Register*, March 22, 2021. https://www.ncregister.com/commentaries/st-nicholas-owen-the-martyred-carpenter-saint-of-the-english-persecution.

Outdoor Leadership (website). "The Power of One: The Story of Telemachus." Accessed February 19, 2024. https://outdoorleaders.com/experiential-teaching-facilitation/the-power-of-one-the-story-of-telemechus/.

Phillips, Francis. "We can learn a lot from St Nicholas Owen, the priest-hole maker." *Catholic Herald*, August 25, 2014. https://web.archive.org/web/20180824101919/http://www.catholicherald.co.uk/commentandblogs/2014/08/25/we-can-learn-a-lot-from-st-nicholas-owen-the-priest-hole-maker/.

Rochford, Tom. "Nicholas Owen." Jesuits (website). Accessed February 19, 2024. https://www.jesuits.global/saint-blessed/saint-nicholas-owen/.

Sutherland, A. "Nicholas Owen 'Little John' Who Paid Highest Price for His Ingenious, Camouflaged Places to Hide." *Ancient Pages*, December 5, 2017. https://www.ancientpages.com/2017/12/05/nicholas-owen-little-john-paid-highest-price-ingenious-camouflaged-places-hide/.

Thurston, Herbert and Donald Attwater, eds. *Butler's Lives of the Saints* (Westminster, MD: Christian Classics).